Advice to
My Daughter

99 Lessons on Love, Life,
Success & Society

Marjory Sheba

Special Edition

To my daughter Asha:

May these vital lessons, combined with your own experiences, empower you to live and fulfil your very best life!

With Love,
Mom

Other books by Marjory Sheba:

- Sometimes You Have to Close Your Eyes to See
- Our Thoughts Are Not Our Own
- Ideals of a Realist

www.MarjoryShebaLive.com

Author Foreword

When we reflect on our lives, many factors come into play. These factors can vary depending on what is currently impacting our thoughts, our reality, and the stage of life we're in. Whether we're teenagers, young adults, middle-aged, or elderly, each phase affects how we perceive and handle our individual experiences and those we create in the relationships we build. Factors like our level of maturity, our emotional and physical well-being, our environment, and even our mood all contribute to the reality we create. We have a choice: we can either let these factors consume us or rise above them with an open mind.

In truth, we embrace our realities in doses, therefore often never learning the lessons that life teaches us all at once. We are brave, cowardly, bold, sensitive, strong and weak- all at various points in our lives! We build our hopes up, kick our fears down, shake loose our doubts- when we let our best selves win. But, in a moment of defeat- become insecure, angry, deeply conflicted and, at times, our worst enemies. Positive words alone cannot restore us to our happy state. It takes more. Some infallible belief or inner conviction must exist to establish a sense of connection with the information we are consuming, feeding our minds, and even uttering out loud. We will have to do more to be and remain truly uplifted within.

Anyone who has ever entered into this whelm of their lives, if they live long or wisely enough, will reach a point where they begin to seek out a deeper meaning for their existence. We want to identify with something greater, ethereal, a more profound purpose of sort. A means to manifest our ultimate desires and wants and achieve a more fulfilling end.

I remember feeling overcome by this need to "Find my purpose" by the time I was 25 years old. I was searching for myself in everything in a quest to understand how my life fits into it all. I arrived, years later, at accepting the fact that our purpose in life is always unfolding, that our biggest self-discovery doesn't happen only from our wins, but from our losses too. And in the end, we can all meet our calling everyday by simply being open to learning, to giving more of ourselves and living a better life.

Marjory Sheba,
Author

TABLE
OF CONTENTS

Introduction

I first became inspired to write this book in 2016, following a long dialogue with my then 13-year-old daughter, Ashadé. As a young divorced and single mother of a blossoming, young teenage girl, I had made time for many a mother-daughter talks like that one and would encourage her to ask questions about whatever she wanted to know. We had moved some 4 years prior away from family and loved ones and settled hours away in a new city where I was to find more opportunities for my career and business. However, that day the conversation had shifted to things in a future time, and how she believes she would handle being in a variety of situations, absent of my presence and help.

We were in my bedroom and she was sat at the edge of my bed, brushing and parting her own hair to braid (a skill she had just begun to perfect). We talked about relationships and why they fail. We discussed college life and deciding on careers. We went on and on about societal expectations, relationships, raising children, going into business and finding the right balance in between. She listened, disagreed at times and had a ton of questions. And, in the hours passing, we laughed, bonded got to understand each other more and felt, without exception, this was our best talk on those topics yet. As we wrapped up the night to go to our respective beds, she asked "Mom, how will I remember all these things we talked about?" I looked at her puzzled by her question, advised her that this is why we have these talks often, and that although she may not remember all of my counsels, they were seeping into her subconscious, still, for when she would most need them. She thought for a while then added "I wish you would put them in a book for me."

There is an African proverb I love that says, "A man who has not prepared his own children for his death, has failed as a father." I have always believed this to be true, and for mothers too! My talks with my daughter, although they may at times have seemed random to her, were always intentional and purposeful. In the days and weeks that passed, I had thought long and hard about my daughter's request and felt it would be a great service to her to fulfill on. I thought also of my younger family members, friends from the community, young women who had come to me for advice through the years and how much they, too, might benefit from such a book. I thought about the heart to hearts I had with my late grandmother, Roseline, and how wonderful it would have been to open a book and revisit those moments and bring to life again her caring words to me. The more I reflected on it, the more I became impassioned with the idea. And, in a short time, I had begun to lay the foundations for the subjects I wanted to address in the book and the lessons I wanted to share. I did not want to rush the process and would take long pauses in between to read, to grow, to live, and manage other aspects of my life.

By late 2019, I had completed the manuscript, but it would take the next couple of years up to now, 2023, before I made a few more additions and edits and felt it was ready for its intended purpose. I was content. Satisfied. Resolved. I thought, parents and guardians from everywhere can share these insights with their own daughters and sons, just as I had with mine, and add the lessons included to those they have learned and experienced. But, even more satisfying, was knowing I was delivering on a promise I made to my daughter, when I took her up on her request and responded, "Yes. I will do just that for you and write that book."

Here is, "Advice to My Daughter: 99 Lessons on Love, Life, Success & Society."

CHAPTER 1:

Lessons on Love
& Relationships

Lesson #1.

CHOOSE YOUR LOVERS CAUTIOUSLY.

Each one leaves a permanent trail.

Everything carries energy. The room you're in. The water you drink. The words you speak. Even the clothes you wear.

In physics, energy is described as "A property of objects which can be transferred to other objects or converted into different forms." But even science struggles to provide one single comprehensive definition of energy because of its many implied forms.

Here, I speak on a spiritual level of energy as a spirit, an aura, an intangible and invisible veil that attaches itself to and becomes a part of everything around us. Spiritual energy lives in every breathing creation, in every human being and animal. Some may refer to it as a certain "vibe" or feeling, like meeting someone and immediately picking up a positive or a negative aura about them.

Every one of us are a beam of energy that we take into every room we enter and every encounter we have. The same is true for the close friendships, relationships and lovers we allow into our lives. There are ties and bonds that we form with every relationship we build that never break. Remnants of energy, unseen effects and spirit trails that linger long after their absence. Sometimes this shows up in our moods, our memories and even in the way we feel when we are alone in those closed space environments, we once shared with them.

Be mindful of the energy you invite into your life, for it can shape your experiences and influence your overall well-being. Seek relationships that uplift and inspire you, where mutual respect, love, and growth are the foundations. Surround yourself with individuals who share your values, aspirations, and desire for emotional and spiritual connection.

Remember that energy is contagious, and the relationships we engage in can either elevate us or drain our spirits. Choose partners who align with your vision, values, and goals, and whose spirit resonates with your own. Look for those who bring out the best in you, who support your dreams and aspirations, and who genuinely care for your well-being.

Be equally attentive of the energy you bring into your relationships. Take the time to cultivate self-awareness and nurture your own well-being. Be mindful of the energy you radiate and strive to be a positive force in the lives of others. Remember that the energy you project has the power to influence and shape the dynamics of your relationships. Understand that not all connections will endure. Some relationships are meant to be temporary, serving as a lesson on your journey of self-discovery. If a relationship no longer aligns with your values, aspirations, or overall well-being, have the courage to release it with love and gratitude for all it has brought into your life. Trust your intuition. Remain discerning in your choices and seek connections that nurture and support your growth. Surround yourself with those whose energy uplifts and aligns with your spirit, and together, you can create a love that is transformative, empowering, and enduring.

Memo to Asha: *My dear, remember the story I shared with you about this one professor I had who felt an immediate connection when he first met his wife? And how they both owned and occupied space in the same timeshare unit, at different times for years, and would learn of this only a year after being together? There is energy in every connection we create, and in every space we occupy we leave a bit of ourselves.*

Lesson #2.

KNOW WHAT LOVE IS AND SETTLE FOR NOTHING LESS.

Love has no border yet maintains restraints.
It flies freely as a mountain bird that daily returns to its nest.
It is a creative energy,
Always moving, always producing,
Always seeking to enhance.
Love is wholesome and self-complete.
It manifests itself in all ways.
It is evident in all things.
If you must ask if it is love, then something significant is lacking.
Where there is love, there is FREEDOM, JOY, and GROWTH.
That is the ultimate proof.

— MSheba

"Love manifests itself in all ways. It is evident in all things." I wrote this poem above a couple of years ago, as part of an opening to a motivational talk I had to give. I remember thinking deeply about what ultimately "Love" as an emotion and expression meant to me and trying my best to capture what I believed was its true essence in a few, meaningful words.

All of us go through life carrying our own interpretations of love. Our conditioning in life began the very day we had consciousness. In part, what we observed about love from our parents, in part what we are taught by the religions we follow and practice. It all plays a part, our culturally inherited morals and values, our formed perceptions and our very own lived experiences- whether correctly or incorrectly interpreted. Those of us who seek earnestly enough and become wiser with time, come to the understanding that Love is a choice, a commitment. That it continually gives in and of itself and finds deep fulfilment in the gratification of others' needs and innate desires.

Love is a principle, not an attraction or feeling. It engages our strongest senses and sentiments (i.e., yearnings, wants, fragilities) to deliver on its quest. We can only truly love when we are made whole within ourselves. When you find true love in someone, you will never need to worry about their complete acceptance or capability to love you- flaws and all.

Memo to Asha: My dear, there will be lessons that take you some time to fully grasp, this one included. I'll admit, I struggled to understand most of what this implies until in my 30's. I was blessed to have been always open to the counsels of those more experienced and wiser than me, and to listening to my own awaken intuition that guided me throughout my teens and 20's. You will make mistakes, more than likely, but if you take heed to this lesson in life- you may spare some of the more consequential ones.

Lesson #3.

YOU'LL NEVER HAVE TO LOOK FOR LOVE IF YOU MAKE ITS COURTS YOUR HOME.

Love thrives in truth and peace, in selflessness and gentleness.
It has a walk, keeps a certain rhythm, and hums a specific tune.

This is a secret known by some of the wisest in our world: You attract ultimately who you are! So much of what we constantly seek in life seems to remain unattainable, to lie outside of us and seemingly out of reach. This is because we haven't learned to first tap into that internal aspect of us that has us drawn to those external things we desire, in the first place. Every feeling, gift, fulfilment we seek comes from a place within us that knows that certain feeling, gift or fulfilment well enough to desire it.

The Kabbalah teaches, in part, that: We yearn for love because we come from love; for peace, because we come from a place of peace. And, just the same, we yearn for God, for our Creator, because we come from God. This surmises in many ways why we as a human species seek to fill those yearnings we have through the formation of various religions, and the practice of meditation and other spiritual rituals. We come from a place of goodness, love and purity- and forever long to find ourselves there again. To be made whole by the very elements we were separated from.

Rumi, a 13th-century Persian poet and theologian, stated: "Your task is not to seek for love, but merely to seek and find all the barriers within yourself that you have built against it." We lose ourselves in carrying out our daily activities, work and responsibilities, all in the name of being productive, bettering our lives, getting ahead, and finding happiness. We take the longer roads; get stuck in a roundabout and waste days and years with ample 'activity' to show for and very little 'productivity'. I believe in a natural flow and order of things. The more we are in alignment with God and nature, the more whole we are, the more we will attract the good things we so earnestly seek that also exist outside of us.

Memo to Asha: If you draw anything out of this passage, let it be this: When you create love for yourself from a place deep within, it will radiate all around you. And it's only that kind of love that will attract the kind of true and lasting love from others that you seek. Make love your home above all.

Lesson #4.

BECOME THE BEST OF YOU, BEFORE YOU CHOOSE THE BEST ONE FOR YOU.

Your quality of life, for the rest of your life depends on it.

Your best, as you will know it and as life will opportune you to become, is an ever-unfolding journey. It is reaching a state where you have put in place, at the very least, the foundational pillars you will need to rely and build on for the rest of your life. You will know you have attained this point by your sense of confidence, level of independence, your emotional and financial endurance and your ability to make difficult decisions, without feeling ill equipped or doubting yourself in the aftermath.

A known adage in the business world is the saying, "Build it and they will come." This does not only reveal the process by which a savvy business owner attracts his or her customers, but also the preparation required to attract the right customers and patrons. A smart entrepreneur will always seek to position his or herself on the side of opportunity: That place where he/she arrives at amassing enough knowledge, resources and information to maintain an upper advantage for their business decisions through a multitude of options.

The same goes for a successful love life. You must first strive to be and attain your best self, and to be sure of three things:

(1). Your all-around (mental, emotional, intellectual etc.) soundness in order to attract your right fit. (2). Your capacity to meet and manage the requirements of said relationship, and (3). Your ability to achieve and sustain a certain quality of life with or without said partner.

Doing this will not only assure you are choosing someone who is qualified for you and is also at their best- but will put you in a better position to love them and care for them as they would have deserved to be.

Memo to Asha: My dear, I've had to put this lesson into application for most of my life. Those long pauses and, sometimes, years I would take in between dating were as a result. We have to learn to deny ourselves the average, the ok, and even the good enough, to go after the best. Choosing to be alone, to better yourself, to focus on your craft, to self-care is a wise and rewarding decision I pray you will always be willing to welcome and celebrate.

Lesson #5.

KNOW WHO YOU'RE WITH AND WHY THEY'RE WITH YOU.

A true partner will stop at nothing to protect you and your interest.

In a relationship, it its crucial to know the essence of your connection to the person you're with and unravel the profound intricacies of their presence in your life. A genuine and lasting partner, characterized by unwavering loyalty, support, understanding etc., exhibits a myriad of qualities that serve as pillars of trust and support. You must grasp an essential understanding of who they truly are and the underlying reasons that bind your paths together before you over invest yourself.

We all have values that we hold dear and being in a relationship should not mean having to compromise them. Take your time to uncover the things that are important to someone you're interested in, asking the pertinent questions, learning about their past, and most importantly observing their behaviors in various situations. Make a list for yourself of key characteristics you wish to see in your ideal partner and review them periodically. Here are a few to be sure to include:

1. **Trustworthiness:** A trustworthy partner is one who consistently proves themselves reliable and dependable. They honor their

commitments, remain consistent in their actions, and uphold their word with unwavering integrity. Trust is the foundation upon which a lasting partnership is built.

2. **Emotional Support:** A true partner stands by your side through the highs and lows of life, offering unwavering emotional support. They lend a compassionate ear, empathize with your struggles, and provide a safe space for vulnerability. They are your confidant and source of solace in times of need.

3. **Mutual Respect:** A key characteristic of an ideal, long-term partner is the mutual respect they hold for you and your individuality. They appreciate your values, opinions, and dreams, fostering an environment where both partners can thrive as unique individuals. They celebrate your accomplishments and treat you with dignity, kindness, and admiration.

4. **Selflessness and Sacrifice:** A devoted partner is willing to make selfless sacrifices for the betterment of the relationship. They prioritize the collective welfare over personal gains and exhibit a genuine willingness to go above and beyond to ensure your happiness and well-being. They are there to support and protect you, even if it means putting their own needs aside.

5. **Communication and Honesty:** Open and honest communication forms the cornerstone of a lasting partnership. A loyal partner fosters an environment where thoughts, feelings, and concerns can be shared without fear of judgment or retribution. They value transparency and actively engage in meaningful conversations to resolve conflicts and strengthen the bond between you.

6. **Shared Values and Goals:** A long-term partner who remains devoted to your journey recognizes the importance of shared values and goals. They align with your vision for the future, as they too are aiming at bettering themselves every day, fostering a sense of unity and collaboration. Together, you build a solid foundation rooted in common aspirations and shared principles.

7. **Unwavering Support and Protection:** A real partner stands as your unwavering protector, willing to go to great lengths to ensure your well-being and safety. They provide a steadfast presence, offering comfort, encouragement, and a sense of security. They champion your dreams and aspirations, always believing in your potential.

Attaining a profound wisdom of knowing your partner's essence and the intentions that bind you must become a priority. A true partner, fueled by loyalty and love, will spare no effort in safeguarding your best interests, embodying the virtues of trust, support, respect, selflessness, open communication, shared values, and unwavering protection.

Memo to Asha: People will seek your attention and closeness for a myriad of reasons, not always with your best interest at heart. Identify and develop the qualities and characteristics of those you want to give access to your life and build with. Make a list and constantly review and analyze it to assure you are always measuring those who desire to enter your life to those standards. This will help you stay on course and be key to your long-term success and happiness overall.

Lesson #6.

TRUE REGRET IS CHANGED BEHAVIOR.

Let nothing else convince you otherwise.

True regret stems from transformed actions. It is not mere words or fleeting remorse that define a genuine reconsideration for our words and actions. But rather the tangible shift in behavior that follows. When we experience regret, it is a signal that we recognize the impact of our choices and actions. However, it is not enough to simply acknowledge our missteps. True regret demands a sincere commitment to change our behavior, to veer away from the path that led us astray.

Empty promises or hollow apologies may temporarily appease, but they hold no weight without genuine transformation. Ultimately, it is through tangible actions and consistent efforts that the echoes of regret can be silenced and replaced with a new course of conduct.

Allow this understanding to anchor your convictions, always. Let the evidence of changed behavior be the litmus test for a true understanding of their infringement and heartfelt remorse. By embodying this principle, you can navigate a path of personal growth and avoid being swayed by empty reassurances or superficial gestures.

Remember, it is through the sincere transformation of our behavior that regret finds its redemption. Embrace this truth and let it guide your actions, for in the realm of remorse, changed behavior stands as the ultimate testament of genuine regret.

Memo to Asha: My dear, may you remember this, always: People will fail themselves, so inevitably they can and will fail you too. While you should always make room for others' mistakes, never allow yourself to make excuses for their lack of real efforts towards wanting to be and stay in your life.

Lesson #7.

LET LOVE WIN.

Life is a constant battle between love and ego.
Love is always willing to say I'm sorry,
Ego always wants to hear it.

Life unfolds as an eternal struggle, a ceaseless conflict between the forces of love and ego. Within this cosmic dance, love radiates its magnanimous essence, while ego seeks validation and affirmation. Amidst this interplay, a profound dynamic emerges. Love possesses the innate capacity to humbly utter the words "I'm sorry," whereas ego relentlessly craves the sweet melody of those very words.

Love, a boundless wellspring of compassion and understanding, stands ready to embrace vulnerability and acknowledge its missteps. It recognizes that erring is an intrinsic part of the human experience and readily offers the healing balm of apology. Love understands that the act of saying "I'm sorry" is not a sign of weakness, but a testament to its strength and resilience. It perceives the transformative power of genuine remorse and strives to mend the fractures caused by its own imperfections.

Conversely, ego, driven by self-importance and a relentless pursuit of validation, yearns to hear those words of apology. It feeds on the perceived victory that comes from someone admitting fault. Ego thrives on the external affirmation of its superiority, eagerly awaiting the opportunity to declare its triumph over love. It revels in the assurance that its own worthiness has been acknowledged, cherishing the moment when love bows down to its demands. Yet, amidst this cosmic battle, the essence of love prevails. It recognizes that true healing arises not from the gratification of ego's desires, but from the sincere and heartfelt expression of remorse. Love understands that the act of saying "I'm sorry" is an act of reconciliation, a bridge that spans the divide between souls. It perceives the transformative nature of genuine apology, for it is in those moments relationships are strengthened, wounds are mended and peace is restored.

Memo to Asha: My child, you will afront situations in life where being willing to be vulnerable and open to a less condemning and more forgiving approach, will prove to be the most beneficial. See to it in those moments you don't lean on your pride alone. Go with your healed heart and let love win.

Lesson #8.

Remember,
LOVE ISN'T DIFFICULT.
People are.

In the tapestry of life, where emotions intertwine and relationships unfold, a simple truth emerges: Love itself is not inherently difficult. It is the intricate nature of human beings that can make the journey of love a complex and challenging one.

In its pure essence, love is a force that flows freely and unconditionally. It is a boundless energy that nurtures, uplifts, and connects us at our core. Love is compassionate, understanding, and accepting. It is a beautiful and effortless expression. Love does not discriminate or withhold its warmth based on external factors.

People, with their unique perspectives, histories, and emotions, bring forth the intricacies that intertwine with love. Our individual experiences, insecurities, and fears can shape the way we give and receive love. Each person carries their own baggage, their own wounds and limitations, which can at times complicate the expression of love. We may find ourselves entangled in the web of expectations, misunderstandings, and communication barriers. Our own insecurities and fears can manifest as walls that hinder the free flow of love.

The interplay of desires, vulnerabilities, and personal growth can present challenges along the path of love. It is within our power to navigate the complexities of human nature, to cultivate self-awareness, empathy, and understanding. By acknowledging our own limitations and being willing to do the work, we can foster an environment where love can flourish.

Memo to Asha: My dear, where there is real love, issues and conflicts between two people will not linger. This is because true love is preceded by a desire for freedom- for yourself and others. A willingness to achieve deep understanding, an openness to learning and a strong determination to realize, lasting joy, peace and continuous growth at all cost.

Lesson #9.

USE YOUR INTUITION.

You may never be told everything you need to know about someone you're with. Not by them nor by others close to them and you. But you have God's guidance, your Intuition and your Intelligence; use them.

I want to share some ancient knowledge with you as it contains a truth that will help you navigate the complex web of relationships. It is this: neither the person you are with nor anyone close to you will ever tell you everything you need to know about them. Even while it might initially appear difficult, I can promise you that you already have the skills and resources to successfully navigate this enormous ocean of uncertainty. Remember first and foremost that you have a divine connection to the Creator, the supreme force, the loving presence that we refer to as God. You have access to wisdom beyond what is known to humans through this sacred relationship. Trust on your spiritual intuition since it is a lighthouse of truth within you. Look inward and find comfort in prayer or meditation when you're feeling uncertain or confused. If you are willing to observe and listen, you will have the answers.

Additionally, value your intuition since it serves as an effective compass that can direct you towards what is right and true. It is that still, small voice inside of you that whispers to you and guides you toward a more profound knowing and understanding. When you interact with people, pay attention to the tiny indications and feelings that occur within you.

Accept knowledge as a gift and foster an interest in learning. With a critical eye, study the words and deeds of individuals around you, never completely relying on what you learn from outside sources. Learn to look past the obvious and explore the depths of compassion and empathy. Do your best to comprehend people's motivations, anxieties, and desires because true understanding can only be found in these depths.

The delicate balancing act between God's direction, your intuition, and your intelligence will, in the end, make your way clear. But, keep in mind, that no amount of wisdom or knowledge can provide 100 percent assurance in issues of the heart.

Keep in mind that life is a tapestry made of threads of enigma and infinite patterns. Accept the journey with an open mind, recognizing that even though you cannot fully understand another person, you can understand yourself. Respect your own goals, objectives, and values and let them serve as the basis for all of your interpersonal interactions.

May you always follow the road of love, kindness, and authenticity, remembering always you are a remarkable creature who is able to build meaningful relationships and handle the complexity of life with elegance.

Memo to Asha: My dear, you have watched me pray before I leave and re-enter the house, over meals that we ate together, have daily meditations and spend ample time by myself in nature. These are all ways to increase your awareness and deepen your intuition. It will serve well in life if you learn to pay attention and listen.

Lesson #10.

KNOW THE TREE. KNOW ITS FRUITS.

A man cannot be to you something he is not to himself. Or give to you that which he doesn't have for himself to give.

When it comes to choosing the right man for you, never make it about the words he speaks, his potentials, or the 'good' intentions he has. Be on guard even with the things he does to impress you. On their own, these are only a fraction of the real picture. But collectively with alertness and combined with time, you can begin to know WHO he really is. You see appearances can last a long while but can be nonetheless still temporary. That's the tricky part. Don't allow yourself to be easily fooled. Too often, it is the most ill-meaning, dishonest and narcissistic people who know best how to 'play' nice to get what they want.

It's important to get to know someone's true character in life before giving them a substantial place in your heart. To appreciate a tree's fruits, just as we must understand a person to realize their potential, we must first understand them. A person's capacity to love, support, and care for you is intricately linked to their perception of themselves. A man will find it difficult to provide you with kindness, empathy, and honesty if he lacks these traits inside himself. It is crucial to pay attention to a person's character, values, and deeds since they speak volumes about who they are on the inside.

Keep in mind that it is not up to you to alter or correct another person. You cannot change a man into something he is not, no matter how much love you have to give. He needs to set off on his own path of personal development. Then and only then will he acquire the traits required to be a sincere and loving companion.

A man can only give you what he has within himself, just as a tree can only produce the fruits that are inside of it. He won't be able to give you the emotional support and stability you need if he lacks emotional maturity. He can find it difficult to contribute to a solid future together if he is not financially stable. It's critical to consider what a person brings to the table and whether those goals mesh with your own.

Cherish yourself and recognize your value. Never accept less than you deserve. Look for a companion who is aware of himself and who has developed qualities that will strengthen your bond. Find someone who has the capacity to support you with all of their love, respect, and compassion. Make good decisions and allow your inner wisdom to guide your heart. Trust in yourself and never forget that you deserve a love that makes your life better in every aspect.

Memo to Asha: My dear, I wish there was a way to assure the good-hearted person I know you to be, to only have positive and caring people come into your life. But, unfortunately, that's not the way of the world we live in. So, you'll have to do your part in filtering through the ones who are there to try to break you and rob your joy. They will come as trials and tests, it's up to you how long you let them last in your life, if you granted them access at all.

Lesson #11.

LEARN TO LOVE OUTSIDE YOUR "BOX".

Maturity in love (and life) is never allowing your familiarities to become your limitations. Too often the limitations we accept and put on ourselves were never created by us in the first place. They are products and ideologies of our childhood conditioning and current environment.

We can see the effects of limitations in our lives when influenced by friends and even from the people around us whom we seldom know- yet have great care for their opinions of us. In all corners of the world, people tend to live a certain way, enjoy a certain type of food, express themselves through a particular fashion or music style. Our very morals are arguably shaped, in a large part, by the beliefs systems we hold, the education (home training) we were bestowed and the cultures we were passed on.

This means, oftentimes we like the things we like simply by association, or because we are exposed to them repeatedly and develop a prejudice for all things that seem to contrast to them in comparison. We develop biases towards things, ideas and individuals we are more willing to accept over others, simply because these things, ideas and individuals have become the preferences and "norms" to the societies we belong to.

Pre-conceived notions about people and assumptions made of anything unknown that is yet proven is denying ourselves a possible life-transforming experience we may go all our years seeking. It is literally building a box for ourselves and choosing to enter and live inside of it, all while claiming the mantra "I am open and receptive to all the good things the Universe has in store for me."

We say we want fulfillment, yet we fear the very journey that will lead us to it. We say we want something more, something better, yet we are afraid to explore the very path that can unlock our blessings in unimaginable ways.

Memo to Asha: When you are ready to explore (a new) love, don't limit yourself to the old roads and ways you are used to. Learn to be open to life, to be receptive, to be slow to judge. Every new encounter is an open possibility to a lifelong friendship and meaningful relationship. The most rewarding encounters often derive from the most unexpected circumstances.

Lesson #12.

HURTING OTHERS AND HURTING ONESELF, GO HAND IN HAND. *Remember that*.

We live in a world where selfishness is considered a right and doing what's good and rewarding for oneself- regardless of how it affects others- is seen as a display of cleverness, strength and intelligence.

We see and accept deception and disappointment as part of the human experience, pain and inner conflict as part of the human fabric. We endure a degree of hurt, dishonesty and disloyalty damp enough to drown in, by the time we make it out of grammar school and have the majority of our life in front of us to live. We engage with and interact with others who offer us little to no solace, and yet continue to impose demands on us.

Much of the ways we learn to live with others have been through our own experience with our families, friends and loved ones. We come to know love by the very people who are positioned to teach us about heartbreak. And, just the same, we heal from our wounds and heartbreaks by the very ones who set out to exploit our good hearts, love and generosity.

No one can cheat another without also cheating themselves: Of time, future blessings, and peace of mind. When someone hurts you or takes from you, they take from and hurt their future too. The wrong they do to you comes back to them in the end. Learn from the pain and let it go. Don't let your heart break; let it only expand.

Memo to Asha: My dear, The Golden Rule of Life tells us that we ought to "Treat others as we want to be treated.". But there is a Platinum Rule which I believe is wiser to follow, and it says, "Treat others as THEY would like to be treated." This means what translates as love and care to you, may not translate the same to someone else. So, if your goal is to be unselfish, kind and show fairness to others, you will need to learn their interpretations of kindness and fairness and willingness to reciprocate.

Lesson #13.

THINK TWICE BEFORE YOU SAY I DO.

Nothing derails your destiny more than to be married to the wrong person.

One of the most important decisions you'll ever make is whether or not to get married, so you should approach it with the utmost caution and thought. Marriage is a sacred union that should enrich your life and provide you with support. It is a relationship based on affection, faith, and common goals. Being married to the wrong person, though, has the greatest ability to sabotage your destiny. Your happiness, personal development, and general well-being can all be significantly impacted by the person you pick to be your life partner.

Before committing to a lifetime of marriage, take the time to get to know your mate. Past the initial awe and butterflies in your stomach phase. Think about their guiding principles and aims. Think about whether your goals are similar and whether you can help each other grow into your best selves.

Keep in mind, my love, that a happy marriage necessitates compatibility, comprehension, and a strong emotional bond. No relationship is perfect but being in the wrong one can cause you to feel unhappy, resentful, and trapped in a life that wasn't meant for you.

Don't rush into marriage if you are unsure or have any misgivings. Spend some time having frank discussions with people in order to get understanding. Ask for advice from the people who care about you and who love you since they may have insightful opinions.

Above all, keep in mind that your fulfilment and happiness are important. You deserve a companion that values and encourages you, someone who travels with you on your path to a successful future.

Memo to Asha: My darling, think carefully before saying "I do" and entering into a binding union with someone. Assure that, among other things, this choice that you make is in line with your future goals and objectives, not just your current situation or theirs. May you find love in a supportive partner who will be true to God, love and believe in you and be ever committed to protecting and bringing out the best in you, every day of your life.

Lesson #14.

ABOVE ALL, LOVE YOURSELF.

In this fast-paced and often chaotic world, it is easy to seek external sources for happiness, validation, and fulfillment. But the greatest gift you can give yourself is the gift of self-love.

Loving yourself is an act of self-care and self-respect. It means recognizing your worth, embracing your uniqueness, and nurturing your soul. When you love yourself first, you cultivate a solid foundation from which all other aspects of your life can flourish.

No drug, no matter how enticing or addictive, can fill the void within your heart. Substances may provide temporary relief or escape, but it cannot replace the deep and lasting contentment that comes from accepting and cherishing who you are. You are a beautiful and remarkable individual, deserving of love and compassion, from both yourself and others.

Similarly, no material possession or person can ever complete you or bring you lasting happiness if you do not first find that within yourself. Ultimately only you can take action to heal your wounds. Relationships are meant to enhance your life, not define it. When you love and value yourself, you attract others who appreciate and value you for who you truly are. Remember, a healthy and fulfilling partnership is built on the foundation of two whole individuals, supporting and uplifting each other.

Prioritize your self-love journey above all else. Nurture your mind, body, and spirit. Practice self-care, embrace your flaws and celebrate your strengths. Treat yourself with kindness, forgiveness, and compassion, just as you would a dear friend. Remember, you are deserving of love, happiness, and all the beautiful things life has to offer.

Memo to Asha: My child, my wish for you as your mother is that you first develop an unwavering love for God and for yourself. May it serve as the compass that leads you to a life filled with joy, peace and genuine fulfillment.

Lesson #15.

NEVER CONFUSE NEEDINESS FOR LOVE.

One is born of fear, the other of freedom.
One gives to possess, the other to empower.
One inflicts suppression, the other inspires
transformation.

Never mistake neediness for love. Understanding the key distinctions between these two emotions is essential because they have the power to substantially influence both the course of your relationships and your own personal development.

Love is an immense and inspiring power that arises from a position of freedom. It is an emotion that comes naturally and is devoid of need or dread. Love fosters a sense of joy, acceptance, and progress in both the giver and the receiver. It is an act of selflessness motivated by a sincere desire to see the other person prosper.

On the other end, neediness develops from a sense of uncertainty and anxiety. It starts from a point of deprivation, where one looks to others for approval, attention, or fulfilment. Possessiveness is a common sign of neediness because it is an attempt to hold onto someone or something in order to satisfy an inner empty. It is a suffocating feeling that can cause suffocation feelings and the deterioration of personal boundaries.

Love inspires change and growth when it is present. It empowers partners to be true to who they are while supporting one another's goals and desires. Love creates an atmosphere of respect, trust, and open communication that enables both partners to grow and prosper together.

On the other hand, neediness causes relationship suppression. Controlling behavior, envy, and a persistent desire for affirmation might result from it. Neediness limits both parties' independence and prevents them from growing personally. A relationship loses its vibrancy as a result, and feelings of reliance and suffocation take its place.

Memo to Asha: This is one lesson that took me years to understand and apply to my life and those around me. Often, as women we can become attached to the people we feel we're needed by. We spring unto our nurturer and mother roles and welcome them further in, taking on weights that were never ours to take on. Neediness doesn't warrant love; it warrants charity.

Lesson #16.

TEMPTATION HEIGHTENS OUR SENSES, TRAPS OUR MINDS AND MAKES OF OUR BEST LOGIC ITS AGENTS.

May you always know what you're giving in to and never lack the courage to walk away.

The pull of temptation has a way of impairing our judgment and luring us in. It has the potential to divert us from our real course and influence us to make decisions that we may come to regret.

When we are under the influence of temptation, our senses are heightened, and our reasoning may be clouded. These are the times when we need to be extra cautious and aware of our behavior. At such times, it will be crucial to stop and consider whether yielding to this temptation is consistent with your beliefs, principles, and long-term objectives. Keep in mind that real strength comes from the courage to withstand temptation when it threatens to take us in a bad direction.

Resisting the appeal and consciously choosing to defend yourself from danger can occasionally be the bravest thing you can do. Trust in your inner fortitude and understand that resisting temptation is a sign of respect for your present self and your future. Remember no human or material thing has power over you, unless you allow it. Stand firm in your values and convictions, even in the face of temptation.

> **Memo to Asha:** I have faith in your fortitude and your capacity to triumph over the challenges life throw at you. Even when you are tempted, maintain your commitment to your principles and convictions. Believe always that you have the power to make decisions that are consistent with your highest self.

Lesson #17.

THERE IS NO GREATER TRUTH THAN LOVE. BECAUSE, IN LOVE, ALL IS PROVEN.

The heart asks the mind, "Is it love?"
The mind answers the heart,
"What was the sacrifice?"

Love is a power that is greater than words and ideologies. It is an experience that is demonstrated via deeds and sacrifice, showing the breadth and authenticity of the experience.

When love enters our lives, it stirs the heart and awakens our emotions. The heart, ever curious, asks the mind, "Is it love?" It seeks confirmation, seeking assurance that the feelings it experiences are genuine and true. In response, the mind carefully considers the question and responds to the heart, "What was the sacrifice?"

You see, love cannot be proven through a mere transitory feeling or a string of meaningless words. It is demonstrated by deeds and offerings. Love takes forgiveness, compassion, and, at times, putting others before oneself. It challenges us to make any sacrifice—large or small—for the welfare and fulfilment of the people we cherish.

Little deeds of kindness, unselfish deeds, and continuous support for those we love are all evidence of love. It comes through in the voluntary sacrifices we make in order to see others prosper. Seek love that is demonstrated by deeds, not just words. Form bonds with those who are equally prepared to also make sacrifices for your happiness and well-being as you are.

Memo to Asha: My dear, never accept flimsy or shallow relationships. Pick a relationship that is based on respect, trust, and sacrifice for one another. Allow your emotions to lead you but, use your head to determine if the love you experience is tested, sincere and long-lasting.

Lesson #18.

CLOSURE IS A GIFT YOU GIVE TO YOURSELF.

Accept it and move on.

Often, we come across events or relationships in life that make us feel incomplete or unsettled. We yearn for resolution, looking for explanations or a sense of completion. True closure, however, does not always come from outside sources. You have the ability to offer yourself this gift.

Closure is a process of inward acceptance and release. It is about achieving inner peace, regardless whether you get any justification or an apology from the person. It is the act of admitting that some things are out of our control and that concentrating on the past prevents us from moving forward in life and from being happy.

When you embrace closure, you free yourself from the burden of carrying emotional baggage. You release yourself from the chains that bind you to the past, allowing yourself to move forward with a lighter heart and a renewed sense of purpose. Closure enables you to create space for new experiences, relationships, and opportunities in your life.

Accepting closure might be difficult because it calls for fortitude and bravery. It might entail extending forgiveness to both yourself and others and realizing that we are all flawed beings traveling down individual paths. It entails letting go of expectations and realizing that not everything will go as planned or hoped for.

Keep in mind that closure is an act of self-care and self-respect, not weakness. It gives you the power to reclaim your own story, define your own happiness, and set off on a path that suits your actual aspirations. You honor your path and yourself, to this point and beyond, by accepting closure.

Memo to Asha: *My dear, my wish for you is that you view closure as a transformational and liberating gift and that your openness to it leads you to a future rich with happiness, new beginnings and endless growth.*

CHAPTER 2:

Lessons on Life &
Challenges

Lesson #19.

ALL OF LIFE IS A TEST.
AND, WE ALL HAVE OUR
CHALLENGES TO MEET.

This simple, yet profound phrase encapsulates a fundamental understanding of life in our world and our individual obligations as we navigate through our journey together.

Life is a vast and intricate tapestry stitched together from threads of happiness and sadness, success and failure, and love and loss. It presents us with a series of trials and tribulations, designed to test our strength, resilience, and character. Each experience, whether grand or seemingly insignificant, is an opportunity for growth and self-discovery.

When we accept these challenges, we transform into the complete spectrum of ourself as we cross each milestone on the path to our own personal change and self-understanding. Remember, difficulties are designed to make us stronger and more resilient, rather than to break us. We all experience difficulties and challenges differently. Whether physically, emotionally, intellectually, or mentally. What counts is how we handle them. Our task is to approach every obstacle with a fearless heart and an open mind because they have the power to reveal abilities that are hidden within you as well as the inner strength and wisdom you need to conquer future difficulties.

It is equally important that we give ourselves occasional permission to find and accept comfort in the help and direction of family members and close friends who genuinely care about our well-being. The bonds we forge with others, built on trust and compassion, provide strength in moments of vulnerability and unity in times of trial.

While you face the challenges of life, keep in mind the value of meditation and introspection. Take a moment to consider the teachings you have been given. What can you take away from the circumstances you run into? How do you learn to develop from them? Adopt a growth attitude and see every obstacle as an opportunity to learn, grow, and comprehend more. Accept the discomfort that comes with growth because it signals achievement and serves as a springboard for one's own development.

You must also understand that life is not only characterized by its trials and tribulations. Embrace the beauty that surrounds you, the moments of joy, laughter, and love. Celebrate your achievements, no matter how small they may seem. Find solace in the little things, because they can help you get through difficult times. Develop your connections, treasure your connections, and make memories that will uplift your spirit along the way.

Always keep in mind that life's challenges are not intended to discourage or demoralize you. They serve as the foundation for developing your character, resiliency, and wisdom. See the growth that comes with each obstacle, ask for advice from those who care, and take on every challenge with courage.

Memo to Asha: *My dear, as you delve deeper into your life, you will realize that no one is immune to hardship. Each person faces their own battles, and what may appear insignificant from the outside can be a monumental struggle within. Let this knowledge inspire compassion and empathy in your heart, my love, and be a gentle reminder to extend kindness and understanding to all those you encounter.*

Lesson #20.

EMBRACE THE GOOD WITH THE BAD.

Life, my love, is a series of experiences that encompass both joy and sorrow, success and failure. It is a tapestry woven with contrasting threads, where the bright hues of happiness are interwoven with the somber shades of disappointment. Each person, regardless of their circumstances, carries their own burdens and navigates through their own challenges. Remember that the weight someone bears may be just as heavy for them as your own burdens are for you.

Embracing the good with the bad does not mean that we passively accept adversity or overlook the blessings in our lives. It means finding the courage to face challenges head-on, to learn and grow from them. It means acknowledging the blessings that surround us, even amidst trials. Remember that it is often through the storms of life that we appreciate the warmth and radiance of the sunlight.

Adversity teaches us resilience, and it also helps us find our inner power. Challenges offer chances for improvement, introspection, and the acquisition of essential life skills. Accept them as lessons to be learned, not as insurmountable challenges. Seek advice and direction from individuals who have overcome difficulty, and let their experiences motivate and inspire you. Remember that the path through life is a delicate dance between good and bad, success and failure. Open your arms to all sides, for it is only through acceptance that we may achieve balance, toughness, and ultimate fulfillment.

Memo to Asha: My dear, as you navigate through life, remember always that you are capable, powerful and protected. Believe in yourself and push forward. You come from a long line of women who drew from their strengths to overcome challenges and thrive in the face of difficulty. You've got this.

Lesson #21.

LIFE IS NOW. DON'T WAIT TO START LIVING. BE PRESENT. SPEND TIME WITH FAMILY. AND ENJOY THE LAZY DAYS.

In the hustle and bustle of daily life, it's easy to get caught up in responsibilities, obligations, and the pursuit of future goals. However, it is essential to pause, take a step back, and cherish the present moment. Be fully present in each experience, whether it is spending time with family, pursuing your passions, or simply enjoying the lazy days.

The time we spend with our loved ones offers us one of the greatest treasures of life. Family bonds are precious and irreplaceable. Make it a priority to carve out quality time to connect, communicate, and create lasting memories with your family. Engage in meaningful conversations, share laughter, and support one another through both the ups and downs of life. These moments of togetherness will enrich your relationships and provide a strong foundation of love and support.

While ambition and hard work have their place, it's equally important to allow yourself moments of relaxation and rejuvenation. Embrace the lazy days, where you can unwind, recharge, and find solace in the simplicity of doing nothing. These moments of rest are essential for your physical, mental, and emotional well-being. Use this time to reflect, meditate, or engage in activities that bring you joy and peace.

Remember that life is not just about achieving goals and accumulating achievements. It is about savoring the journey, finding joy in the little moments, and nurturing the relationships that matter most.

Memo to Asha: *My daughter, as you endure the complexities of life, remember that you are never alone. Don't wait for tomorrow to start truly living. Embrace the beauty of each day and create a life filled with love, laughter, and fulfillment. Spend quality time with family and find joy in the simplicity of life's lazy days. By doing so, you will cultivate a life that is rich, meaningful, and rewarding.*

Lesson #22.

BE CAREFUL WITH YOUR THOUGHTS.

Your mind will always believe everything you tell it.
Feed it hope. Feed it truth. Feed it love.

Our mind is like a fertile garden waiting to be nurtured. The thoughts you cultivate within it have the power to manifest into your reality. Feed your mind with hope, my dear, for hope is the beacon that guides you through the darkest of times. In moments of uncertainty or doubt, let hope be the fuel that propels you forward, igniting your dreams and aspirations.

Embrace the truth, my precious one, for the truth is the compass that leads you on the path of authenticity. Seek honesty within yourself and the world around you, for it is through truth that you find clarity, wisdom, and personal growth. Feed your mind with love. Love is the nourishment that sustains your spirit, empowering you to radiate kindness, compassion, and empathy. Fill your thoughts with positivity, for the words you speak to and about yourself have a profound impact on your well-being. Watch carefully what you think, believe, and say, for the power of your own self-perception is greater than any words others may use to criticize you or bring you down.

You are a magnificent being, my love, with unique talents, strengths, and beauty that deserve to be celebrated. Speak words of encouragement and kindness to yourself, for they hold the power to uplift your spirit and nurture your growth. Embrace your flaws and imperfections, for they are part of what makes you beautifully human. Treat yourself with the same love and compassion you would extend to a loved one or close friend, for you are deserving of your own care and affection.

Memo to Asha: My precious child, remember that your thoughts have the ability to shape your reality. They create the lens through which you perceive the world and influence the choices you make. Cultivate a mindset of positivity, resilience, and gratitude, for it is through these perspectives that you can overcome challenges and find joy in even the simplest of moments.

Lesson #23.

LIVE IN YOUR TRUTH.

In a world that often places emphasis on external validation and societal expectations, it can be tempting to mold yourself into someone you think others want you to be. However, when you sacrifice your authenticity to fit into someone else's ideals, you deny yourself the opportunity to fully embrace your uniqueness and the incredible potential that lies within.

Authenticity is a beacon that attracts genuine connections, opportunities, and experiences into your life. It is a reflection of your values, passions, and innermost desires and the foundation upon which a fulfilling and meaningful life is built. When you live in your truth, you radiate an aura of confidence and self-assurance that captivates those around you. Your true self is what resonates deeply with others and allows for genuine, meaningful relationships to flourish. Furthermore, living in your truth opens doors to unforeseen blessings that may have otherwise passed you by; you attract opportunities that align with your current needs, wants, values and aspirations. By embracing who you truly are, you create a path that leads you to experiences and endeavors that genuinely fulfill you. It is these unexpected opportunities that can shape your life in ways you may have never imagined.

Remember that your truth is unique to you. Although it may differ from what others expect or desire for you, embrace your individuality and have the courage to stand firm in it. Do not fear the judgment or opinions of others. Surround yourself with people who love and support you for who you are, not for who they want you to be. The relationships you cultivate based on mutual respect and acceptance will bring you immeasurable joy and fulfillment. So, live according to your values and pursue the passions that ignite your soul. Your authenticity is a gift that sets you apart and allows you to make a profound impact on the world.

So, live your life for you and not to impress others. Your unique authenticity is a precious gift that should never be compromised. Embrace it, nurture it, and let it guide you on the remarkable path that awaits you.

Memo to Asha: My dearest, let your truth be the vibrant thread that weaves through every moment. Embrace your authentic self, unapologetically and wholeheartedly. Trust in the journey that unfolds when you honor your truth, for it will lead you to a life filled with purpose, joy, and genuine connections.

Lesson #24.

ASK, DON'T ASSUME. EXPLAIN, DON'T COMPLAIN. COMMUNICATE, DON'T CONDEMN. PASSIVE-AGGRESSIVENESS DOESN'T SERVE ANYONE.

When faced with a situation that requires communication, my love, be direct in expressing your thoughts, feelings, and needs. Avoid making assumptions about others' intentions or expecting them to read your mind. Instead, ask for clarification or express your concerns openly and honestly. By doing so, you create an environment of open dialogue, where misunderstandings can be addressed, and relationships can grow stronger.

Complaining seldom leads to productive outcomes. Instead of dwelling on problems or venting frustrations, strive to explain your perspective and concerns in a constructive manner. Seek to understand the underlying causes of any issues and offer potential solutions.

Communication is a powerful tool that should be used to build bridges, not walls. Avoid condemning or attacking others with your words, as it only leads to defensiveness and further misunderstandings. Instead, choose to communicate with empathy, respect, and understanding.

Share your thoughts and emotions, while being mindful of the impact your words may have on others. Effective communication requires active participation from all parties involved. Encourage others to express themselves honestly and be attentive and receptive when they do.

Let directness be your guiding principle. Ask questions when in doubt, seeking clarity and understanding. Explain your thoughts and feelings without resorting to complaint or blame.

Memo to Asha: My daughter, remember by embracing direct communication and rejecting passive-aggressiveness, you empower yourself to build authentic relationships, foster understanding, and create a harmonious environment where others' needs are acknowledged and respected.

Lesson #25.

YOU ARE NOT WHAT HAPPENS TO YOU.

Life is a journey with ups and downs, successes and setbacks, happiness and sadness. You can come into situations along the way that make you feel vulnerable or put your fortitude to the test. It's important to keep in mind, though, that neither your value nor your future are determined by these circumstances. You are more than just the result of the situations or things that happen in your life. Your identity is actually shaped by the concepts you decide to accept and cultivate within yourself.

It is the beliefs you create within yourself, my love, that become the foundation of your identity. The thoughts and interpretations you hold about your experiences build the perceptions you hold of yourself and the world around you. Therefore, choose your beliefs wisely and consciously.

Life is filled with infinite possibilities. Your past does not dictate your future. You have the power to redefine yourself, to rewrite your narrative, and to create a life aligned with your dreams and aspirations. Embrace the belief that you are capable, resilient, and deserving of all the beauty and joy life has to offer. Your future is not determined by your history. You have the ability to redefine who you are, change the course of your story, and design a life that is in line with your goals and desires.

Let rid of any self-limiting ideas that may have developed as a result of trying circumstances. Give up the idea that any one incident, error, or failure defines who you are. Instead, focus on the qualities, values, and dreams that resonate deep within your soul. Cultivate self-belief, self-compassion, and self-love. Embrace the truth that you are a constantly evolving being, capable of growth and transformation.

Memo to Asha: My dear daughter, remember this: You are never what happened to you- good or bad. You are a brilliant, individual spirit with boundless potential and the ability to define your past and direct your own course in life. Embrace the belief that you are the author of your own story, and let your experiences serve as steppingstones on the path to a life of meaning, fulfillment, and joy.

Lesson #26.

LIFE CAN BE A SLIPPERY SLOPE. BEWARE OF YOUR BETRAYALS. BEWARE OF YOUR OFFENSES.

No deed, good or bad, is ever lost to the wind. Everything is accounted for; everything balances out in the end.

Every action you take has consequences that reverberate through the course of your life. Lies, acts of betrayal, whether intentional or not, can cause great damage to a relationship and have longstanding, irreparable effects. Similarly, offenses, even while unintentional, have the power to wound and harm others. The words we speak and the actions we take can leave deep scars on the hearts and souls of those around us. In the grand scheme of life, every action finds its place in the balance. The good and the bad, the acts of kindness and the moments of transgression, all contribute to the intricate web of cause and effect. While it may seem that some deeds go unnoticed or are forgotten, the universe holds a sense of justice that seeks equilibrium. It is not for us to judge the timeline or the precise outcome of this balancing act, but to understand that every action, in some way, contributes to the tapestry of existence.

Remember that cultivating awareness and accountability in your actions is a testament to your character and integrity. Be mindful of the impact of your choices and strive to be a beacon of light in the lives of others. Choose kindness over cruelty, and to treat others with respect and compassion. Embrace empathy, forgiveness, and understanding as you navigate the complexities of human interactions.

Life is a journey of growth and learning, my beloved daughter. Embrace the lessons that come from both the triumphs and the challenges. Be accountable for your choices, seek forgiveness when necessary, and endeavor to make amends when you have caused harm. By doing so, you contribute to the healing and restoration of relationships, fostering a world built on trust, compassion, and understanding.

Memo to Asha: Beware of your betrayals, my dear, and beware of your offenses. Let your actions be guided by the knowledge that every deed is accounted for and contributes to the balance of life. Strive to leave a positive impact, to uplift others, and to be a source of light in the world you're creating.

Lesson #27.

BE GRATEFUL FOR WHAT YOU HAVE AND MAKE THE MOST OF EVERY MOMENT.

Life is fragile, and time is a precious gift. Every breath we take is a reminder of our existence and the opportunities that lie before us. Yet, it is all too easy to fall into the trap of complaining, allowing our minds to focus on what we lack rather than appreciating what we have. But, as we use our breath to complain about life, someone else is taking in their last.

This poignant truth is not meant to instill fear or sorrow, but rather to awaken us to the beauty and richness of each passing moment. When we cultivate gratitude, we shift our perspective and open our hearts to the abundance that surrounds us. We begin to see the simple joys and blessings that we may have overlooked—the warmth of a loved one's embrace, the laughter shared with friends, the beauty of nature unfolding before our eyes.

Gratitude is a transformative force. It allows us to find contentment and fulfillment in the present moment, rather than always seeking more or dwelling on what is lacking. It reminds us of the interconnectedness of our lives and the countless blessings that are often taken for granted. However, gratitude alone is not enough. We must also make the most of every moment.

Life is not a passive experience; it is an invitation to fully participate and engage with the collective of existence. Each moment holds within it the potential for growth, learning, and the creation of lasting memories. Embrace the opportunities that come your way, take risks, and step outside of your comfort zone. Allow yourself to be present and fully immersed in the richness of life.

You have the power to shape your own experiences. Choose to live with intention and purpose. Pursue your passions, cultivate meaningful relationships, and invest your time and energy in activities that bring you joy and fulfillment. Embrace the challenges that come your way as opportunities for growth and resilience.

Memo to Asha: My dear, always be grateful for what you have and make the most of every moment. Embrace the precious gift of life you've been given and cherish every breath. Let gratitude guide your perspective and seize the opportunities that present themselves. Remember that life is a tapestry to be lived fully, with open hearts and grateful spirits.

Lesson #28.

WE BECOME WHAT WE CHOOSE.

The woes and the wins we experience in life
Are ultimately the results of the decisions we make
every day.

Life is a journey filled with countless crossroads, where we are faced with choices both big and small. These choices shape the path we walk and the person we become. They determine whether we embrace growth, seize opportunities, and manifest our dreams, or succumb to stagnation and limitation. Every decision we make carry consequences that ripple through time, creating a chain of events, leading us to different outcomes and shaping our future. The woes we face are often the result of unwise choices, moments when we veered off the path of our authentic self, true values and aspirations.

It is essential to approach decision-making with mindfulness and intention. We must pause and reflect on the consequences of our choices. Consider how they align with our values, goals, and the person we aspire to be. No decision is without risk or uncertainty. Life is inherently filled with unknowns, and we cannot predict all the outcomes of our choices. However, we can choose to embrace the growth mindset, viewing challenges as opportunities for learning and development. When faced with adversity, ask yourself, "What can I learn from this? How can I grow stronger through this experience?"

We must recognize that our choices not only impact our own lives but also the lives of those around us. The decisions we make can have far-reaching effects on our loved ones, our communities, and even the world at large. The power to shape our destiny lies in your hands. Embrace the responsibility that comes with it and make choices that align with our beliefs and purpose.

Memo to Asha: My child, choose wisely, be brave, and embrace the power of your choices. May you be ever courageous in pursuing your dreams, resilient in the face of setbacks, and compassionate in your interactions with others. And may with each decision, you shape the course of your life, becoming the person you were meant to be.

Lesson #29.

DO JUDGE A BOOK BY ITS COVER.

Just be sure to read its contents.

You may have heard the saying, "Don't judge a book by its cover." But, I believe, rather, that the opposite is essential. Human nature is inherently equipped with protective filters and instincts that guide us in our interactions and decisions. These instincts have evolved over time as a means of self-preservation and discernment. They provide us with initial impressions or gut feelings about people, places, or things. These impressions are not to be disregarded but rather acknowledged and examined.

When encountering someone or something new, it is natural for us to form initial judgments based on appearances, behaviours, or circumstances. These judgments serve as a preliminary assessment and can influence our actions and level of trust. Although, it is important to remember that judgments alone do not tell the whole story.

The true essence of a person or situation lies beyond the surface. Just as a book's cover may offer hints about its contents, it is essential to go beyond those initial impressions and delve into the heart of the matter. Take the time to read the contents, observe and study to truly understand and appreciate the depth and nuances that lie within.

Approach your judgments with a balanced perspective. Trust your instincts, but also be open to the possibility that there is more to discover. Avoid snap judgments that are solely based on appearances or limited information. Allow for the possibility of growth, change, and understanding. Engage in active listening, meaningful conversations, and seek to understand the motivations, experiences, and values of those you meet.

Keep in mind that judgment and discernment are inherent aspects of life. They serve as protective mechanisms and help us navigate the complexities of our world. But true understanding and connection can only be achieved when we go beyond initial judgments and take the time to explore the contents within.

Memo to Asha: My child, embrace the wisdom of discernment. Trust your instincts and be mindful of the impressions you form. Be open to expanding your understanding and embracing the richness that lies beneath the surface. Seek to discover the true essence of individuals you cross on your journey. It is through this exploration that you will truly grow, connect, and flourish.

Lesson #30.

MIND HOW YOU LIVE AND LIVE SO IT MATTERS.

A life is a terrible thing to waste.

One of the keys to living a meaningful life is to cultivate your gifts and talents. Each of us possesses unique abilities and strengths that, when nurtured and developed, can bring immense fulfillment and joy. Consider the following to help you identify your passions, explore your interests, and expand on your continuous learning and growth:

Further your education and expand your knowledge, for it is through learning that we gain the tools we need to make a greater impact.

Travel, it broadens our perspectives and deepens our understanding of the world. Explore different cultures, immerse yourself in new experiences, and embrace the beauty and diversity that exists beyond our comfort zone. Travel allows us to connect with people from all walks of life, fostering empathy, compassion, and a global mindset.

Volunteering is a powerful way to make a difference in the lives of others and create positive change. Find causes that resonate with your values and dedicate your time and energy to them. Whether it is serving the less fortunate, advocating for the environment, or supporting a local community project, your efforts can bring fulfillment, hope, joy, and tangible benefits to those in need.

Write a book, your thoughts and experiences hold a unique perspective that can inspire and enlighten others. Share your stories, insights, and wisdom with the world, as your words have the power to uplift, educate, and spark change.

Launch an organization that addresses a need or problem in life or your community. Channel your passion, skills, and resources into creating solutions that bring relief and support to those who need it most.

Lead a movement or cause to make a lasting impact. Identify an issue that ignites your passion and rally others around it. Advocate for justice, equality, and positive change. Be a voice for the voiceless and work towards creating a more inclusive, compassionate and thriving society.

A life well-lived is not solely measured by personal accomplishments but by the impact we have on others and the world around us. Live with intention, embrace your passions, and strive to make a difference, no matter how big or small. It is through the collective efforts of individuals like you that we can create a better world for future generations.

Memo to Asha: My dearest, may you seize each day with purpose, cultivate your gifts, and utilize your time, God-given abilities and talents for the best. Keep furthering your education. Travel. Volunteer. Write a book. Launch an organization that meets a dire need. Lead a movement or cause. In all, aim always to leave a positive imprint wherever you go.

Lesson #31.

SOMETIMES SAYING "NO" TO OTHERS IS THE BEST WAY TO SAY "YES" TO YOUR FUTURE.

It is natural to want to please others and be there for those around you. However, it is crucial to recognize that your time and energy are limited resources. Sticking to your priorities and focusing on activities that can genuinely change your position in life requires the ability to say "no" when necessary. This may mean declining invitations, turning down certain requests, or setting boundaries to protect your time and energy. It is not about being selfish, but rather about valuing yourself and your future. Every "yes" you say to someone or something means saying "no" to something else, including your own goals and personal well-being.

You don't have to be everywhere or support everything. It is far better to invest your time and efforts in a few meaningful projects that align with your vision and values than to spread yourself too thin. Being busy does not necessarily equate to being productive. Every scattered attention and energy devoted to numerous endeavors can prevent you from making significant progress in any of them.

Time is a precious and non-renewable resource. Once it is gone, it cannot be replaced. Therefore, it is vital to guard your time and only exchange it for activities and commitments that truly reflect your worth and contribute to your growth and fulfillment.

When faced with requests or opportunities, pause and reflect on whether they align with your spirit, objectives, aspirations and overall goals for your life. Ask yourself, "Will this contribute to my personal growth? Will it bring me closer to my dreams? Does it align with my priorities?" If the answer is no, have the courage to decline gracefully. Saying "no" to others is not a reflection of your worth or character, but rather a testament to your commitment to living a more purposeful and aligned life.

Memo to Asha: My dear, your future is shaped by the choices you make every day. Embrace the power of saying "no" when it serves your best interests and focus on what truly matters. Surround yourself with supportive individuals who respect your boundaries and understand the value you place on your time. Cherish your time and say "yes" to opportunities pave the way for a future filled with growth, fulfillment, and meaningful accomplishments.

Lesson #32.

THERE ARE NO MISTAKES, NO COINCIDENCES. ONLY LEARNING OPPORTUNITIES.

Each circumstance, encounter, or challenge is intricately woven into the fabric of our journey, guiding us towards becoming the best version of ourselves. Life does not simply happen "to" us, but rather "with" and "from" us. Even when faced with difficult situations, there is always a hidden provision for greatness, waiting to be discovered and embraced.

Comparing our life to others or dwelling on past regrets serves no purpose. Each individual's path is unique, and every person faces their own trials and tribulations. Instead of succumbing to the trap of comparison or regret, we should focus on the lessons and opportunities that arise from our experiences.

Remember that it is during our most challenging moments that we have the greatest potential for growth and transformation. Adversity can be the catalyst that propels us to greatness, and setbacks can serve as steppingstones to success. Never allow your trials or circumstances to define you or limit your potential. Embrace them as opportunities to rise above, to cultivate resilience, and to become more of what you are meant to be.

The underdog, often underestimated and faced with overwhelming odds, can unexpectedly emerge as the biggest winner. Their journey is a testament to the indomitable human spirit and the power of perseverance. It is through the crucible of trials that strength, determination, and character are forged.

You are not limited by your trials or circumstances. Believe in yourself and trust that every experience you encounter is an opportunity for growth and self-discovery. Embrace the challenges, setbacks, and even the moments of uncertainty, for they hold within them the seeds of greatness. Have faith in your ability to overcome, to learn, and to evolve.

Memo to Asha: My dear, life is a journey of continuous learning and growth. Every experience, whether uplifting or challenging, holds within it the potential for greatness. Know that you are capable of rising above any circumstance and becoming the person you are meant to be.

Lesson #33.

BE MORE CHARITABLE.

There isn't someone you wouldn't love,
if you knew their whole story.

It's easy to make judgments or form opinions about others based on skewed or limited information and superficial interactions. However, true understanding and empathy arise when we take the time to truly know someone, to understand their struggles, their triumphs, and the complexities of their journey. Every person has a unique story, filled with joys and sorrows, victories and defeats.

By being charitable, we open our hearts to the beauty of human diversity and recognize the shared humanity that connects us all. Instead of quick judgments or prejudices, seek to understand and empathize with others.

Every individual is fighting their own battles, facing their own fears, and striving to find meaning and happiness. Our goal should be to approach each person we encounter with an open mind and a willingness to listen, to learn, and to appreciate their unique perspective. A charitable heart allows us to extend kindness, love, and support to those around us, regardless of their background or circumstances.

When we make the conscious effort to understand someone's whole story, we gain a deeper appreciation for their struggles and triumphs. We realize that their actions and behaviors are influenced by their experiences, their upbringing, and the challenges they have faced. This understanding foster compassion, forgiveness, and a genuine desire to uplift and support others.

Embracing charity also means extending a helping hand to those in need. Actively seeking opportunities to make a positive impact in the lives of others. We can volunteer our time and skills to organizations that support causes close to our hearts. Show kindness to strangers, lend a listening ear to those who are hurting, and offer a helping hand to those who are less fortunate. Small acts of charity can create a ripple effect of goodness and bring joy and hope to those who need it most.

Memo to Asha: My dear, always remember the power of love, understanding, and compassion as a tool with which to navigate your life. Practice charity towards others, and in doing so, you will not only enrich their lives but also find profound fulfillment and growth within your own heart.

Lesson #34.

WE ATTRACT AND ALLIGN WITH PEOPLE AND EXPERIENCES WE ULTIMATELY NEED.

Take account of the lessons you are being taught and continue to rise.

The people and experiences that come into our lives are not mere coincidences but rather meaningful connections and synchronicities. They serve as mirrors, reflecting aspects of ourselves that need attention or growth. Sometimes, they challenge us, push our boundaries, and expose us to new perspectives. Other times, they bring joy, support, and love, reminding us of the beauty and interconnectedness of humanity.

It is crucial to approach each interaction and experience with an open heart and a willingness to learn. Pay attention to the lessons being presented to you, even if they come in the form of challenges or hardships. These lessons are not meant to break you but to build resilience, strength, and wisdom within you.

When you encounter difficult or challenging situations, take a moment to reflect on the underlying lessons they hold. Ask yourself what you can learn from these experiences and how you can grow from them. Likewise, cherish the positive connections and experiences that come your way. Surround yourself with individuals who uplift, inspire, and support your growth. These people will serve as beacons of light along your journey, guiding you towards becoming the best version of yourself.

Life is a continuous journey of learning and self-discovery. Each person you meet, each experience you have, plays a vital role in shaping your character and helping you evolve. Embrace the opportunities for growth and development and have faith that you are attracting and aligning with what you ultimately need to become the person you are meant to be.

Memo to Asha: My dear, my hope for you is that you continue to elevate and attract to your life all that is aligned for your growth and happiness. Remain open to the lessons and embrace the connections and experiences that come your way. May you apply wisdom in every encounter and continue to evolve into the magnificent person you are destined to become.

Lesson #35.

BE BOLD. FACE YOUR FEARS AND TAKE CHANCES.

This life we have requires courage, and we only live it once.

Fear can often hold us back from pursuing our dreams and taking risks. It whispers doubts in our ears, tempting us to stay within our comfort zones. But true growth and fulfillment lie just beyond the boundaries of fear. It is when we summon the courage to face our fears head-on that we unlock our true potential.

We ought to be unafraid to step outside of our comfort zone. We should take chances, pursue our passions, and explore the depths of our capabilities. Every successful person have had to face their own fears and taken risks along their journey. They have embraced discomfort and uncertainty, knowing that it is through these experiences that true growth occurs. Life is about embracing the uncertainties and challenges that come with venturing into the unknown, for it is within those moments that we discover our strength and resilience. Each step we bravely take in the face of the unknown is a testament of our unflinching courage and determination.

While taking chances may come with risks, it also opens the door to remarkable opportunities and life-changing experiences. Embracing new experiences, seizing the moments that excite you, and not being afraid to pursue the path less traveled. Remember that some of the most rewarding and transformative journeys are born from boldness and a willingness to take calculated risks.

Mistakes and setbacks are an inevitable part of life's journey. Do not let the fear of failure deter you from pursuing your dreams. Embrace failure as a steppingstone to success, for it is through setbacks that we learn valuable lessons, develop resilience, and gain the wisdom needed to navigate future challenges.

Memo to Asha: *My dear, may you embrace the opportunities that come your way, even if they seem daunting or uncertain. Remember that you have the power within you to create the life you want and will be fulfilled by.*

Lesson #36.

GUARD YOUR HEART. GUARD YOUR HEALTH. GUARD YOUR PEACE. GUARD YOUR WEALTH.

Always.

Guarding your health means taking care of your physical, mental, and emotional well-being. Nourishing your body with nutritious food, engaging in regular exercise, and getting enough rest and sleep. Take time to prioritize self-care and engage in activities that bring you joy and rejuvenation. Pay attention to your mental and emotional health by seeking support when needed, practicing mindfulness, and cultivating healthy coping mechanisms. Remember that your health is your most valuable asset and taking proactive steps to care for it will enable you to lead a fulfilling and vibrant life.

Equally important is guarding your peace. In a fast-paced and often chaotic world, it is essential to create boundaries and cultivate a sense of inner calm and tranquility. Surround yourself with positive influences and environments that uplift and inspire you. Prioritize activities and relationships that bring you peace and avoid those that drain your energy or cause unnecessary stress. Practice mindfulness and seek inner balance through practices such as meditation, journaling, or spending time in nature. Remember that your peace of mind is a precious gift that you should safeguard fiercely.

Above all, guard your worth, which encompasses your wealth. Recognize your inherent value as a unique and remarkable individual. Never allow anyone or anything to undermine your sense of self-worth or diminish your confidence. Surround yourself with people who appreciate and uplift you, and distance yourself from those who seek to belittle or devalue you. Set healthy boundaries in your relationships and stand up for yourself when necessary. Remember that you deserve love, respect, and kindness, both from others and from yourself. Never settle for anything less than you deserve.

Memo to Asha: My dear daughter, always remember that you have the power to shape your own life. Guarding your health, peace, and worth is not a one-time task but a lifelong commitment. Make conscious choices that prioritize your well-being and ensure that your actions align with your values and aspirations. Trust in your own worthiness and never settle for anything less than what brings you genuine happiness and fulfillment.

Lesson #37.

DON'T DESPISE YOUR SMALL BEGINNINGS.

Every triumphant story is marked with moments of struggle, perseverance, and growth. No inspiring tale of victory would be complete without the chapters that detail the hardships and obstacles overcome. It is through these trials and tests that character is built, skills are honed, and resilience is developed.

Where you are right now is a necessary part of your journey towards success. Embrace your current circumstances with gratitude and humility, knowing that this is where true growth must happen. Small beginnings provide fertile ground for learning, self-discovery, and skill development. They offer the opportunity to lay a strong foundation and build a solid framework for future success.

Do not be discouraged by the apparent limitations of your current situation. Instead, view it as an opportunity to learn, adapt, and grow. Embrace the challenges that come your way, for they hold valuable lessons and insights that will shape you into the person you are meant to be. Remember that greatness is not achieved overnight, but through consistent effort, perseverance, and a willingness to learn from every experience. Continue to maintain a positive perspective and focus on progress rather than on the outcome. Celebrate even the smallest victories and milestones along the way. Recognize that every step forward, no matter how small, brings you closer to your goals. Patience and perseverance are key virtues that will guide you through the ups and downs of your journey.

> *Memo to Asha:* Always remember, my dear, that success is not defined by where you start, but by the continuous determination, resilience, and growth you exhibit along the way. Embrace your small beginnings with gratitude, knowing that they are an integral part of your journey towards realizing your dreams and becoming the person you aspire to be.

Lesson #38.

CENTER YOUR LIFE AROUND PURPOSE.
NOT POPULARITY.

It can be tempting to seek validation and acceptance from others, to conform to societal expectations and pursue what is popular. However, true fulfillment and happiness come from aligning your actions and choices with your sense of purpose and staying focused on your course, even if it means saying no to friends and deviating from the crowd.

Saying no is a powerful act of self-care and self-preservation. It allows you to prioritize your time, energy, and resources on the things that truly matter to you. Remember that you don't have to over-explain yourself or justify your decisions to others. Your dreams, aspirations, and goals are unique to you, and it's okay to prioritize them above pleasing everyone else. Resist the pressure to conform to others' definition of fun and fulfillment. Society may dictate that endless nights of partying and socializing are the epitome of enjoyment, but that may not align with your values and aspirations. Fun can take many forms, and it is essential to explore and embrace what brings you genuine joy and fulfillment. Whether it's spending a night alone, engaging in creative pursuits, embarking on a road trip, traveling, or completing an exciting task, prioritize activities that resonate with your sense of purpose and bring you a deep sense of satisfaction.

Centering your life around purpose means living with intention and striving to make a meaningful impact in the world. Identify what truly matters to you and set goals that align with your values and passions. Nurture your talents, pursue your passions, and continuously seek personal growth and self-improvement. Remember that popularity and external validation may be fleeting, but the fulfillment that comes from living a purpose-driven life is long-lasting and deeply satisfying.

Trust your own judgment and intuition. Stay true to your authentic self and don't be swayed by the opinions and expectations of others. Your path in life may be different from those around you, and that is perfectly okay. Embrace your individuality and have the courage to follow your own unique journey, even if it means venturing into uncharted territory.

Memo to Asha: My dear daughter, centering your life around purpose is a lifelong commitment that requires self-reflection, courage, and determination. Stay focused on your course, pursue what brings you joy and fulfillment, and never be afraid to say no to things that don't align with your goals. Remember, it is your life to live, and your purpose to fulfill.

Lesson #39.

BE GRATEFUL FOR IT ALL.

What's left. What stayed. What's on the way.

Life is full of changes and transitions, and sometimes we may lose or let go of certain things or people along the way. However, amidst those changes, there are always things that remain—a solid support system, cherished relationships, cherished memories, and the lessons learned. These are the foundations upon which you can continue to build and grow.

Next, be grateful for what has stayed in your life. Some relationships, opportunities, or circumstances endure and stand the test of time. These are the blessings that continue to enrich your life and bring you happiness and gratification. Whether it's long-lasting friendships, a loving family, a stable career, or a passion that has remained ignited within you, express gratitude for these constants in your life. They are the sources of strength and stability that provide a sense of continuity and comfort.

Lastly, be grateful for what's on the way. Life is an ever-unfolding journey, and there are endless possibilities and opportunities that lie ahead. Embrace the future with open arms and a grateful heart. Be excited for the new experiences, relationships, and adventures that are yet to come. Approach them with a sense of anticipation and appreciation, knowing that each new step holds the potential for growth, joy, and discovery.

Gratitude is a powerful practice that allows us to appreciate and find meaning in what we have. It is a mindset that brings contentment, joy, and a deep sense of fulfilment. Learning to cultivate it in all aspects of our life allows us to find beauty and meaning in both the ups and downs. It shifts our focus from what is lacking to what is present, from what has been lost to what remains, and from what we desire to what we already have. When we appreciate and nurture what remains, we reinforce the pillars that will support us as we move forward.

Memo to Asha: My dear, as you journey through life, make gratitude a daily practice. Take moments each day to give thanks for all that you are and have. Let gratitude be the lens through which you view the world, and it will bring you immense joy, peace, and fulfilment.

Lesson #40.

STOP DOUBTING AND START DOING.

This life you have is a blessing.
No one can live it for you, except you for yourself!

You have been blessed with the gift of life, a precious and unique existence that is yours to live. No one else can live it for you or determine your path, except yourself. This realization should ignite a fire within each of us, a determination to make the most of every moment and make a positive impact in the world.

Doubt can be a crippling force that holds us back from reaching our full potential and experiencing the richness of life. It's natural to feel uncertain or fearful when embarking on new ventures or pursuing your dreams. However, it's important to remember that growth and success lie on the other side of our unsureness.

Instead of dwelling on what could go wrong or worrying about the opinions of others, focus on what you can achieve and the fulfillment that awaits you. Trust in your abilities and believe in your potential. Surround yourself with positive influences and support systems that uplift and encourage you. Seek inspiration from those who have overcome their own doubts and accomplished great things.

This life you have is a precious gift, and it is up to you to make the most of it. it's not enough to simply dream and hope for a better future. Action is what brings dreams to life. Break down your goals into manageable tasks and start taking consistent action towards them. Embrace the challenges, embrace the opportunities, and embrace the journey. Celebrate your progress, no matter how small, and let it motivate you to keep moving forward. Trust yourself, believe in your abilities, and let your actions speak louder than any doubts or insecurities.

Remember, you are capable of greatness. Don't let doubt hold you back from embracing the fullness of life and reaching your true potential. Start doing, start taking action, and watch as your dreams unfold before you.

Memo to Asha: My dear, don't allow doubt to consume you. Stay encouraged and motivated. Let go of hesitation and continue to take meaningful steps towards your dreams and aspirations.

Lesson #41.

MAKE PEACE WITH YOUR PAST.

It can overshadow your present.

Being burdened by unresolved emotional baggage from the past can impede you from completely embracing the present and making clear, peaceful progress in the future. While it's important to recognize and deal with any hurt, regrets, or disappointments you may have gone through, concentrating on them endlessly can prevent you from leading a happy and fulfilled life. We are the people we are today as a result of the experiences we've had in the past, both good and bad. It is crucial to avoid letting the past overshadow the present and prevent us from moving forward and finding happiness, even if it is normal to carry the lessons and memories of the past with us.

Not forgetting or dismissing your experiences is not the same as finding peace with them. It is acknowledging what has occurred, extending forgiveness to all involved, including yourself, and figuring out how to go forward with a sense of renewed peace and freedom. You can let go of the burdens that are holding you back and fully appreciate the present moment through this journey of healing and self-discovery.

Reflect on the lessons you have learned from your past experiences, for they have shaped your wisdom and strength. Use them as steppingstones towards personal growth and self-improvement. Remember that you have the power to create a different narrative for your life, one that is not defined by the shadows of the past but illuminated by your resilience and determination.

Seek support from trusted friends, family, or professionals if needed. Talking about your past, expressing your emotions, and gaining different perspectives can provide clarity and help you gain a deeper understanding of yourself. Engage in self-care practices that nurture your mind, body, and soul, such as meditation, journaling, or engaging in hobbies that bring you joy. These activities can foster healing, self-reflection, and self-discovery. You'll discover that your history no longer has any influence over you once you come to terms with it. You can approach the present with a fresh feeling of liberation and opportunity.

Memo to Asha: My dear, you deserve to be happy and at peace. By making peace with your past, you allow yourself to fully embrace the beauty and potential that each present moment holds. Free yourself from the shadows of the past and step into the light of the present with an open heart filled with gratitude, forgiveness, and love.

Lesson #42.

YOU DON'T ALWAYS GET WHAT YOU WANT. BUT IF YOU STAY IN ALLIGNMENT, LIFE WILL ALWAYS GIVE YOU WHAT YOU NEED.

In a world filled with desires and aspirations, it's important to remember that life has its own way of guiding us towards what is truly meant for us. It may not always align with our immediate wants and wishes, but it aligns perfectly with our higher purpose and growth.

When you stay in alignment, you are living in tune with your values, passions, and inner wisdom. You make choices and take actions that are true to yourself, even when they may not conform to societal expectations or the desires of others. This alignment brings you closer to your authentic self and opens the door for opportunities and experiences that are aligned with your highest good.

Sometimes, what we think we want may not be what we actually need. The experiences we have may not always be easy or comfortable, but they are essential for our personal and spiritual development. Embrace them with an open mind and heart, knowing that they are meant to shape you into the person you are destined to become.

By staying in alignment, you cultivate a sense of trust and surrender to the greater flow of life. You release the need for control and allow life to unfold naturally. This doesn't mean being passive or resigned; it means actively participating in the present moment and making choices that align with your values and aspirations, while remaining open to the wisdom of life's unfolding.

Life has a way of providing exactly what we need at the right time. If we trust in the process, even when it seems challenging or uncertain, in the end, we will realize that what we truly needed was far more profound and transformative than what we initially wanted.

Memo to Asha: My dear, learn to embrace the gifts and lessons life presents to you, trusting that staying in alignment will always lead you to a life filled with purpose and joy. Be patient and resilient, knowing that life's plan for you is far greater than any specific desires you may have. Stay true to yourself, follow your intuition, and embrace the journey with gratitude and grace.

Lesson #43.

LIFE IS SHORT.
LOVE HARDER.

Love is a force that transcends boundaries and elevates the human experience. It is the ethereal connection that binds us to others, forging bonds that withstand the test of time. It is the profound affection we hold for our family, the unwavering loyalty we have for our friends, and the passionate devotion we share with our partners.

In the face of life's impermanence, we must seize every opportunity to express our love and affection. Take the time to tell your loved ones how much they mean to you, for kind words have the power to uplift and nurture the human spirit. Show acts of kindness, extending a helping hand to those in need, for love knows no boundaries and embraces the collective human experience.

However, love is not without its challenges. It requires vulnerability, compassion, and a willingness to navigate the complexities of human relationships. It means embracing forgiveness and understanding, recognizing that we are all flawed beings striving for growth and connection. Love compels us to put aside our differences and cultivate empathy, forging deeper connections that transcend superficial barriers.

In the face of adversity, let love be your guiding light. When confronted with anger or resentment, respond with compassion and seek understanding. Love has the power to heal wounds, mend broken relationships, and restore harmony where discord once reigned. Cherish each moment, for they are fleeting and irreplaceable. Embrace love as a guiding force in your life, allowing it to shape your actions, decisions, and relationships. Let love be the driving force behind your endeavors, infusing your every pursuit with purpose and meaning.

> *Memo to Asha:* My dear, may you love with depth and intensity, recognizing that the brevity of life calls for us to immerse ourselves fully in the transformative power of love. Embrace it in all its forms, radiating kindness, compassion, and understanding to all those you encounter. Let love be the legacy you leave behind, a testament to a life well-lived.

Lesson #44.

EVERY OPPORTUNITY YOU MISS, EVERY LIE YOU TELL, EVERY PROMISE YOU BREAK, EVERY WRONG YOU DO ROB A PIECE OF YOUR FUTURE.

It may be easier to blame external factors like pre-destiny, family curses, or bad luck for the challenges we face in life. However, we must recognize that it is our own decisions and behaviours that have a significant influence on our blessings and the direction our lives take.

Every opportunity you miss, every lie you tell, every promise you break, and every wrong you do carries consequences that can rob a piece of your future. It may seem tempting in the moment to take shortcuts, make dishonest choices, or neglect your responsibilities. However, these actions have a way of catching up with us, affecting not only your present but also your future prospects.

Your future is not predetermined by some external force, but rather shaped by the choices you make and the values you uphold. Each decision you make and each action you take has a ripple effect on your path ahead. By acting with integrity, honesty, and responsibility, you pave the way for a future filled with blessings and opportunities.

Your words hold power. The promises you make are a reflection of your character and integrity. Breaking those promises not only damages the trust others have in you, but also hinders the potential for future opportunities. Strive to keep your word, honor your commitments, and be true to your promises. Your integrity will lay the foundation for a future built on trust and reliability.

Do not underestimate the power of your actions and inactions. Even the smallest of deeds can have a profound impact on your life's trajectory. Choose kindness, compassion, and generosity in your interactions with others. These qualities not only enrich your relationships but also create a positive energy that attracts blessings and opportunities.

Do not allow setbacks or failures to define you. Learn from them, grow stronger, and persevere. Take responsibility for your mistakes, make amends when needed, and use these experiences as a guide towards personal growth and wisdom.

Memo to Asha: My dear, you have the power to shape your life through your words, actions, and choices. It is within your hands to increase your blessings, create a positive future, and overcome any obstacles that come your way. Believe in yourself, embrace accountability, and strive to live a life aligned with your values and aspirations.

Lesson #45.

WHEN LIFE GIVES YOU LEMONS, MAKE CHAMPAGNE.

And leave the whole world wondering how you did it.

Life is full of ups and downs, and it is during the challenging moments that our true strength and resilience shine through. Instead of succumbing to despair or allowing setbacks to define you, choose to embrace a mindset of possibility, innovation, and determination. Seeing every obstacle as an opportunity for growth, learning and problem-solving.

The ability to turn something negative into something positive requires a shift in perspective and the willingness to think outside the box. It means not being confined by limitations or conventional expectations. Tap into your creativity, resourcefulness, and inner strength to find innovative solutions and turn adversity into an advantage. Believe in your own abilities and trust in your capacity to overcome obstacles. It may require hard work, perseverance, and consistency, but the rewards can be immense and extraordinary.

Don't be discouraged by the doubters or skeptics who may question how you turned a difficult situation into a profitable one. Instead, let their wonder serve as a testament to your strength, determination, and ability to rise above adversity. Use their disbelief as motivation to push yourself even further and continue striving for greatness.

Believe that you have within you the power to create your own reality and shape your own destiny. When life throws lemons your way, see them as opportunities for growth and transformation. Embrace the challenges, unleash your creativity, and let your resilience and determination shine through. By facing challenges head-on, "Making champagne out of lemonade," and finding unique ways to navigate through your hardships, you will leave a lasting impact and inspire others with your resilience and success.

Memo to Asha: My dear, when life gives you lemons, I pray you let your spirit soar and find the strength within you to transform those challenges into opportunities, leaving the whole world in awe of your ability. May you rise above any difficulty and achieve greatness. May every triumph you have serve as a source of hope and inspiration to those around you, encouraging them to rise above their own challenges and find the extraordinary within every ordinary.

CHAPTER 3:

Lessons on Faith & Spirituality

Lesson #46.

WHEN IT SEEMS EVERYBODY HAS THE ANSWER, GO TO GOD FOR YOURS.

When faced with the multitude of answers and solutions the world may present to you, seeking guidance from God is essential and dire. While others may offer their perspectives and advice, it is important to remember that true wisdom and guidance come from a higher power.

The world often bombards us with countless opinions and information, it can be easy to feel overwhelmed and confused. It is during these times that turning to God becomes even more crucial. He is the source of all knowledge, wisdom, and understanding. Through prayer, meditation, and a deep connection with your spiritual beliefs, you can tap into His divine guidance and find the answers you seek.

The world may offer you solutions that seem appealing or logical on the surface, but without the guidance of God, they can lead to confusion, wasted time, and even failure. Within you lies a reliable compass—the inner spirit and voice that is connected to God. This inner guidance is a gift that allows you to navigate through life's challenges and make decisions aligned with your values and true desires. It is a voice that speaks softly but powerfully, guiding you towards what is right and meaningful. Relying solely on external advice and opinions can lead you astray from your true path and purpose.

Learning to trust and follow your inner spirit requires cultivating a deep sense of self-awareness, mindfulness, and spiritual connection. Take time to quiet the noise of the world and listen to the whispers of your heart. Through prayer, meditation, and reflection, you can develop a stronger connection with God and recognize His guidance when it presents itself. God has a cleat plan for you, and through prayer and meditation, He can provide the answers and wisdom you need when you seek Him. Trusting your inner spirit and following God's words may not always align with popular opinions or societal expectations, but it will grant you inner peace and lead you to a life of success and gratification.

Memo to Asha: My daughter, as you endure the complexities of life, remember that you are never alone. God is always with you, ready to provide you with the answers and guidance you seek. Cultivate a deep relationship with Him, trust your inner spirit, and follow the path that is illuminated by His divine light. In doing so, you will find clarity, peace, and fulfillment in your journey.

Lesson #47.

REMAIN IN TUNE WITH GOD AND STEADFAST ON YOUR JOURNEY.

Everyone else is simply trying to find their own way.

When you seek the opinions of others, you may be inundated with a myriad of misdirected responses, each offering their own perspective and thought. But it is important to remember that opinions are subjective and influenced by individual experiences, beliefs, and biases. Instead of relying solely on the opinions of others, consider their track record and the results they have achieved in their own lives. Often, those who are quick to offer advice may not have the practical experience or success to back up their words.

Amidst the clamor of others' advice on your life, learn to turn to God and inward, and listen to the quiet guidance of your own intuition, for it is there that you will find the truth that resonates with your soul. Trust your spirit and follow the path that aligns with your values, passions, and purpose. Remember that life is too precious to live according to the bias, judgments and limited knowledge of others-no matter how well meaning. Seek the counsel of God, for in His divine wisdom, you will find unwavering guidance and solace for a secured and successful future.

As you encounter various voices and opinions along your journey, remember that not all advice is created equal. Some may come from a place of genuine care and wisdom, while others may be driven by personal agendas or limited perspectives. It is through spiritual discernment that you can differentiate between the two, allowing you to make decisions that resonate with your authentic self.

Cultivating spiritual discernment involves nurturing a deep connection with your inner spirit and developing a relationship with your higher power, God. Take time for quiet reflection, prayer, and meditation to attune yourself to the wisdom and guidance that flows from within. By grounding yourself in spiritual practices, you open yourself up to receiving divine guidance and insight, enabling you to make choices that align with your true purpose and values.

At times, you may encounter conflicting advice, and it is during these moments that your spiritual discernment becomes even more crucial. Trust in your inner guidance, rooted in your connection with a higher power, and let it lead you towards the choices that resonate with your soul's journey. By honing your spiritual discernment, you will navigate the complexities of life with wisdom, clarity, and grace. Your ability to distinguish between the advice to embrace and the advice to respectfully reject will be a guiding light on your path to personal growth, and spiritual fulfillment.

Memo to Asha: My dear, may you always stay true to God and yourself, and have faith in the journey that lies ahead. Trust in the guidance of God's loving spirit, let go of the need for external validation and live a life that is authentic to your own calling, desires and aspirations.

Lesson #48.

BE CAREFUL WHAT YOU BELIEVE AND ACCEPT AS TRUTH.

Limiting beliefs can be a significant obstacle in our lives. They are often ingrained in us through societal conditioning, past experiences, or the influence of others. These beliefs can create self-doubt, fear, and a sense of limitation, holding us back from reaching our full potential.

Recognizing and challenging these limiting beliefs is the first step towards personal growth and transformation. Question the beliefs that no longer serve you and ask yourself if they are based on truth or if they are simply the result of religious conditioning or false narratives. Replace these limiting beliefs with deep spiritual knowledge that elevates, enlightens, gives you confirmation and offers clarity and room for growth.

It is crucial to seek truth and knowledge from reliable sources. Remain curious and open-minded, willing to explore different perspectives and consider alternative viewpoints. Engage in critical thinking, research, and reflection to expand your understanding and challenge any assumptions or beliefs that may be holding you back.

Remember that you have the power to shape your reality through the beliefs you hold. Choose to believe in your inner Guide, your gifts, your abilities, and your power. Embrace beliefs that empower you, inspire you, and align with your true essence. Believe in your capacity for growth, resilience, and success.

Surround yourself with individuals who uplift and support your growth. Seek out mentors, teachers, and friends who challenge you to expand your horizons and embrace new possibilities. Engage in personal development practices such as reading, learning, and self-reflection to continually expand your knowledge and challenge your beliefs. By being discerning in what you believe and accept as truth, you take control of your own narrative and create a foundation for personal growth and success. Everything you are and everything you will become begins with your belief system. Choose beliefs that empower you, inspire you, and align with your true potential.

Memo to Asha: My dear, always strive to be discerning when it comes to what you believe and accept as truth. Our beliefs shape our reality and influence the choices we make, the actions we take, and the outcomes we experience in life. Be ever mindful of the beliefs you hold, weigh and question each one to ensure they serve your highest good.

Lesson #49.

KNOW WHAT YOU WANT
AND SPEAK IT INTO EXISTENCE.

The mind is a powerful tool that is intricately connected to the vastness of the universe. Your thoughts and words have the ability to shape your reality and manifest your desires, significantly. What you focus on and consistently affirm becomes your truth. Therefore, it is crucial to align your thoughts and words with what you truly want to create in your life.

Speak your desires into existence with clarity and conviction. Clearly define your goals, aspirations, and dreams. Affirm them daily, both verbally and through your thoughts. Believe in their possibility and feel the emotions associated with achieving them. By consistently affirming and visualizing your desires, you send a powerful message to the universe, signaling your readiness to receive and manifest your dreams.

Cultivating a positive mindset and guarding against negative thoughts and self-doubt is vital. Be mindful of the words you speak about yourself and your dreams. Replace self-limiting beliefs with empowering affirmations that reinforce your worthiness and potential. Speak words of victory, prosperity, and positivity, even in the face of challenges or setbacks. Remember, that you hold the key to unlocking the abundance and blessings that await you. By knowing what you want in life and speaking it into existence, you tap into the infinite possibilities and resources of the universe. Trust in the process and believe that all of heaven is conspiring to support your journey.

Surround yourself with positive influences and individuals who uplift and inspire you. Seek out mentors, coaches, and friends who believe in your dreams and encourage your growth. Surrounding yourself with a supportive network can amplify the power of your thoughts and words, creating a powerful synergy that propels you towards success.

Know that you have the power to overcome any obstacle or roadblock that may come your way. Stay focused on your goals and maintain a steadfast belief in your ability to achieve them. With every word you speak and every thought you think, you are shaping your reality and co-creating your destiny. Speak with conviction and watch as the universe responds to your unwavering faith and positive affirmations. Know what you want in life, speak it into existence, and embrace the limitless possibilities that await you.

Memo to Asha: My dear, embrace the incredible power that lies within your words and thoughts. The desires and dreams you hold in your heart have the potential to become a reality. Be certain of what you want and speak it over your life, daily, with unwavering faith and positivity.

Lesson #50.

YOU WERE BORN WITH THE DREAMS YOU HAVE TO FULFILL THEM FOR YOUR BETTERMENT AND THE BETTERMENT OF OTHERS.

From the moment you took your first breath, you were filled with dreams and aspirations that are uniquely yours. These dreams are not random, but rather a divine calling meant to be fulfilled for your betterment and the betterment of those around you.

You were born with a purpose, and it is your responsibility to honor that purpose and work towards fulfilling your dreams. Prosperity is not just a wish; it is a mandate from God. You have been blessed with the potential to achieve greatness, and with that blessing comes the obligation to take action. Fulfilling your destiny is not just about personal gain, but also about contributing to the well-being of your community, your family and future generations. Your dreams are interconnected with the dreams of others, and by pursuing them, you create a ripple effect of positive change in the world.

Never shy away from the pursuit of prosperity, for it is not selfish or materialistic. Embrace your dreams with passion and determination. True prosperity encompasses spiritual, emotional, and financial well-being. It empowers you to live a life of purpose, joy, and abundance, allowing you to make a positive impact on the lives of those around you.

To fulfill your dreams and secure your legacy, you must take action. Dreams without action are like seeds without water; they wither away without bearing fruit. Set clear goals, make a plan, and take consistent steps towards their realization. Do not let fear or self-doubt hold you back. Embrace challenges as opportunities for growth and learning.

As you embark on your journey to fulfill your dreams, remember that you are never alone. God has bestowed upon you the strength, wisdom, and resources needed to overcome any obstacle. Trust in His guidance and surrender your worries to Him. Have faith that He will lead you to the path that aligns with your purpose.

While the road to fulfilling your dreams may not always be smooth, every step you take brings you closer to your destiny. Stay persistent and resilient in the face of adversity. Believe in yourself and your abilities. The world may challenge you, but with a strong sense of purpose and determination, you can overcome anything.

Memo to Asha: My dear, you were born with dreams for a reason. Embrace them, nurture them, and take the necessary steps to fulfill them. Prosperity is your birthright, and it is time to claim it.

Lesson #51.

WE ATTRACT TO OURSELVES WHAT WE MANIFEST WITH OUR WORDS AND THOUGHTS: PUBLICLY OR PRIVATELY; GOOD OR BAD.

There is a principle that may appear simple on the surface, but its implications are profound. It is the understanding that we attract into our lives what our words and actions manifest, regardless of whether they are witnessed publicly or transpire in the privacy of our thoughts and hearts. The energy we emit through our thoughts, words, and actions directly influences the circumstances and experiences we encounter.

When our intentions are pure and our words are kind, compassionate, and filled with love, we set into motion positive vibrations that draw forth harmonious relationships and abundant blessings. Conversely, if our thoughts are negative, our words are harsh, or our actions are driven by selfishness and ill-intent, we unwittingly invite discord and hardship into our lives.

It's important to recognize that the state of our external reality is not arbitrary or coincidental. It is a reflection of our inner spiritual condition. Our relationships, our achievements, and even our struggles are mirrors that reveal the essence of our being. They offer valuable insights into our spiritual alignment and the energy we emit into the world.

In understanding this truth, it is crucial to release the impulse to assign blame or attribute external circumstances to factors beyond our control. Instead, we must embrace personal responsibility and acknowledge that the quality of our relationships, the success we attain, and the challenges we face are direct consequences of our spiritual state.

This realization may initially be challenging to accept, for it demands that we take an honest inventory of our thoughts, words, and actions. It requires us to examine the motives behind our choices and assess whether they align with our highest values and aspirations. However, it is in this self-reflection and introspection that we discover the power to effect positive change.

By consciously cultivating positive thoughts, speaking words of kindness and affirmation, and engaging in actions that uplift and empower ourselves and others, we can recalibrate our spiritual alignment. This intentional shift in energy will, in turn, attract more fulfilling relationships, propel us toward greater success, and infuse our lives with harmony and abundance. No blame is relevant in this process.

Remember that you possess the power to shape your reality through your thoughts and actions. Embrace personal accountability, and align yourself with the energy of love, compassion, and integrity. By doing so, you will magnetize positive experiences and forge deeper connections with others. It is not about dwelling on past mistakes or shortcomings but rather about embracing personal growth and embracing the infinite potential within you.

Memo to Asha: *My daughter, changing deep-seated patterns and beliefs takes time and consistent effort. Watch your words, beware of the thoughts you entertain. Allow yourself the space to grow, learn, and evolve, knowing that each step forward brings you closer to the life you desire.*

Lesson #52.

LIVE AS YOU BELIEVE.

Spirit was made to fly, to be free.
What good is achieving this human experience,
if you never dance your own dance or sing your own song?

Imagine a bird with magnificent wings, created to soar high above the world. How tragic it would be if that bird chose to remain grounded, never taking flight nor experiencing the exhilaration of gliding through the boundless sky. In the same way, your spirit was made to fly, to explore the vast expanse of possibilities and express the unique essence that is you.

Living as you believe means honoring your values, following your dreams, and embracing your passions. It means having the courage to dance to your own tune, to sing your own melody, and to create a life that resonates with the very core of your being. It means embracing your individuality and celebrating the beauty of your authentic self.

In a world that often seeks to impose its expectations and conformity upon us, it takes great strength and conviction to live according to our own beliefs. But the rewards are immeasurable. When you live in alignment with your true self, you radiate a magnetic energy that attracts opportunities, connections, and experiences that align with your purpose. You become a beacon of inspiration, lighting the way for others to embrace their own uniqueness.

It is essential to remember that this journey of self-expression and authenticity is not always easy. You may face criticism, judgment, or resistance from those who do not understand or appreciate your choices. But do not let these external voices dim the light within you. Trust in your own intuition and inner guidance, for they will always lead you towards the path that is meant for you.

Memo to Asha: Remember, my dear daughter, that you are here for a reason. You have a unique purpose to fulfill, and the world is waiting for the gifts that only you can offer. Embrace your individuality, spread your wings, and let your spirit soar. Dance to your own tune, sing your own melody, and create a symphony of life that is uniquely yours.

Lesson #53.

SOMETIMES THE LOVE YOU NEED, IS ONE ONLY GOD CAN GIVE.

As human beings, we often seek love and support from others. We form deep bonds with family, friends, and romantic partners, and these relationships bring us joy, companionship, and a sense of belonging. However, there are moments when the love we need goes beyond what any human can offer.

In those moments, turn to God with an open heart and surrender your needs, desires, and struggles to Him. God's love is vast and all-encompassing, beyond the limitations of human understanding. He knows your deepest longings, your pain, and your joys. He listens to your prayers and offers solace, guidance, and comfort in ways that no human can.

You can experience the unconditional and unwavering nature of God's love wherever you are in life. He is always there for you, ready to extend His grace and compassion. When you feel alone, misunderstood, or in need of divine intervention, turn to Him in prayer, meditation, or simply through heartfelt conversations. Pour out your thoughts, hopes, and fears to Him, and trust that He is listening and responding in ways that are best for your highest good. Remember that God's love is not limited by human imperfections or constraints. He sees you for who you truly are, with all your strengths and vulnerabilities, and loves you unconditionally. His love provides solace, healing, and guidance beyond measure. Open your heart to receive His love and allow it to fill the spaces within you that no other love can reach.

In seeking God's love, you will find a deep sense of peace, reassurance, and purpose. His love will nourish your soul, bring clarity to your journey, and strengthen your faith. It is a love that transcends all human limitations and brings you closer to the divine essence within yourself.

Memo to Asha: My dearest, never underestimate the power of God's love in your life. Allow it to guide you, uplift you, and bring you peace. Let your heart be fully fulfilled by the divine presence of God.

Lesson #54.

FIND YOUR PEACE IN ANY STORM.

It's the ultimate secret to a happy life.

Life is filled with storms—moments of chaos, uncertainty, and hardships. These storms can be overwhelming and can threaten to disrupt our inner peace. However, it is within these storms that we have the opportunity to discover our true strength and resilience.

Finding peace in any storm begins with cultivating a spiritual life and fostering a deep and secure relationship with God. Through prayer, meditation, and the practice of connecting with the divine, you can tap into a source of unwavering love, guidance, and peace that can transcend any earthly struggle.

In times of turmoil, it is comforting to know we can turn to God with an open heart, surrendering our fears, worries, and burdens to Him. We can seek His guidance, wisdom, and comfort, knowing that He is always there to listen, support, and uplift us.

Build a daily spiritual practice that nourishes your soul, whether it be through reading sacred texts, engaging in prayer, or spending time in quiet contemplation. Nurture your relationship with God by deepening your understanding of His teachings and incorporating them into your daily life. Seek to embody the qualities of love, kindness and forgiveness that are at the core of His message. Allow His presence to permeate every aspect of your being, guiding your thoughts, words, and actions.

Through a spiritual life and a secure relationship with God, you can find solace and strength in the midst of any storm. Trust in His divine plan and have faith that He is always working for your highest good, even in the face of challenges or setbacks. Surrender your worries and anxieties to Him, knowing that He is capable of turning every difficulty into an opportunity for growth and transformation.

As you cultivate your relationship with God, you will discover a profound sense of peace that surpasses all understanding. This peace will anchor you amidst life's storms, providing you with the strength, clarity, and resilience to navigate through any adversity. It will become a guiding light, illuminating your path and infusing every moment of your life with a sense of purpose and meaning.

Memo to Asha: My dear, your spiritual connection and relationship with God are precious gifts that can bring you immeasurable peace, happiness, and fulfilment. Nurture this connection, lean on His love and guidance, and watch as your life becomes a testament to His grace and wisdom.

CHAPTER 4:

Lessons on Success & Money

Lesson #55.

SUCCESS IS A CHARACTER.

You can recognize it from afar, absent of any glory.
It embraces ambition but despises greed.
It celebrates strength but rejects arrogance.
It is crude in nature but respects its laws.
It sees no limitations yet applies limits.
And, above all, it is honest, disciplined and wise.

Success emanates an aura of quiet confidence, commanding respect and admiration from afar. It exudes a certain gravitas that captivates hearts and minds, drawing people towards its magnetic presence. It stands as a testament to the triumph of determination and perseverance, an inspiration to all who encounter its essence. Ambition runs through its veins, propelling it forward on the path of growth and achievement. Yet, success is not tainted by the toxic allure of greed.

Strength defines the character of success, encompassing not only physical prowess but also mental fortitude and emotional resilience. It stands tall in the face of adversity, weathering storms with unwavering resolve. But success is not marred by the arrogance that often accompanies triumph. Instead, it wears humility as a crown, recognizing that true strength is rooted in empathy and compassion.

Success walks hand in hand with integrity, guided by an unyielding commitment to upholding moral values and ethical principles. It navigates the world with unwavering honesty, shining a light on the path of righteousness. It knows that true accomplishment stems from a foundation of trust and transparency, inspiring others through its unwavering integrity.

While success envisions boundless horizons and limitless possibilities, it understands the importance of boundaries and discipline. It recognizes that focus and wise choices are essential for harnessing its full potential. Success applies the reins of discernment, channelling its energy and resources in ways that yield the greatest impact. It understands that discipline is the gateway to unlocking its truest potential.

Wisdom permeates every fiber of success's being, illuminating its path and guiding its choices. It cherishes the pursuit of knowledge and continuous growth, understanding that true success lies not in complacency but in the unquenchable thirst for understanding.

As you embark on your journey towards success, remember that it is not a solitary pursuit but an intricate dance with this extraordinary character. Embrace ambition tempered by contentment, strength intertwined with humility, and discipline guided by wisdom. Align your values and choices with the embodiment of success, and you will witness its transformative power unfold in your own life.

Memo to Asha: My dear, may the character of success inspire and guide you to leave an indelible mark on the world, not only through accomplishments but through the virtues and principles you embody.

Lesson #56.

Success is a narrow road on which one must BE WILLING TO GO ALONE.

The journey to success is not always a crowded highway bustling with companions and cheerleaders. It is often a solitary path, where you must rely on your own strength and resilience to navigate the challenges that lie ahead. It is a road that demands unwavering commitment, perseverance, and self-belief.

Being willing to go alone on this narrow road means embracing independence and self-reliance. It means having the confidence to trust in your own abilities and intuition, even when others may doubt or question your choices. It requires the willingness to step out of your comfort zone, take risks, and chart your own course, even if it means leaving behind the familiar and venturing into the unknown.

Walking this narrow road can be daunting at times. There may be moments when doubt creeps in, and you question whether you made the right decision to venture alone. But remember that it is on this path that you truly discover your inner strength, resilience, and capacity for growth.

When you walk the narrow road to success alone, you have the freedom to define your own vision and pursue your dreams without compromise. You can make decisions based on your own values and aspirations, unburdened by the expectations or opinions of others. It is a path that allows you to fully embrace your individuality and unleash your true potential. While it may seem lonely at times, being willing to go alone on this narrow road opens up opportunities for self-discovery, self-mastery, and personal growth. You become intimately acquainted with your strengths and weaknesses, and you develop the resilience to overcome obstacles on your own terms. You learn to rely on your inner resources and intuition, honing your decision-making skills and building confidence in your abilities.

Embracing the willingness to go alone does not mean shutting out support or guidance from others. It simply means that you are the primary driver of your own journey, responsible for your own choices and actions. Seek out mentors, advisors, and like-minded individuals who can offer wisdom, support, and encouragement along the way. Surround yourself with a strong support network that understands and respects your path.

Remember that walking the narrow road requires courage, determination, and the willingness to embrace solitude when necessary. Embrace the challenges and uncertainties that come with this path, for it is on this road that you will uncover your true potential.

Memo to Asha: My dear, I pray you always find the strength and resilience within yourself to navigate the narrow road of success with unwavering determination. And may the lessons and triumphs you experience along the way inspire others to embrace their own unique paths to success.

Lesson #57.

USE YOUR STUBBORNNESS FOR SUCCESS.

Embrace your stubbornness as a shield, filtering out the noise of nay-sayers, quitters, and doubters. Tune out their discouraging words and disbelief, for their limited perspectives and fears should never define the boundaries of your dreams. Let your determination be the compass that guides you towards what others deem impossible.

By remaining steadfast in the face of adversity and opposition, you cultivate a resilience that propels you forward. Your stubbornness becomes a driving force, pushing you to overcome obstacles and reach new heights. It serves as a constant reminder of your unwavering commitment to your goals and aspirations.

Remember, my dear daughter, that throughout history, great achievements were often born out of stubbornness and a refusal to accept limitations. It was the stubbornness of inventors, explorers, and visionaries that allowed them to push past boundaries and bring about remarkable change. Embrace this quality within yourself and let it ignite the fire of determination that fuels your pursuit of success.

However, it is important to channel your stubbornness wisely. Let it guide you towards perseverance and tenacity, but also remain open to learning, growing, and constructive feedback. Be discerning in distinguishing between constructive criticism and baseless negativity. Success is not achieved in isolation. Use your stubbornness as a shield, but not as a barrier to personal growth and understanding. Surround yourself with individuals who support and uplift you, who believe in your potential and encourage you to reach for the stars. Seek out mentors and like-minded individuals who inspire you to be your best self. Their guidance can help shape your path and provide invaluable insights along the way.

As you harness your stubbornness for success, remain true to your convictions and never let the doubts of others dim your inner light. Trust your instincts, follow your passion, and hold fast to your dreams. Remember, with an unwavering resolve and determination, you have the power to overcome any obstacle and achieve what others perceive as impossible. Let your stubbornness become a driving force that propels you forward on your journey to success.

Memo to Asha: My child, may your stubbornness be tempered with humility and an open mind, and may it fuel your pursuit of greatness. Believe in yourself, my dear daughter, and never let anyone or anything extinguish the flame of determination that burns within you.

Lesson #58.

STAY MOTIVATED. DREAMS AND DEDICATION MAKE A POWERFUL SUM.

Always be on the hunt for whom you've yet to become!

Motivation serves as the driving force behind your actions and fuels your pursuit of greatness. It is the spark that ignites your dreams, pushing you to take the necessary steps towards their fulfilment. Embrace this inner fire, nurturing it with passion, perseverance, and a relentless pursuit of personal growth.

Dreams have the power to shape your destiny. They inspire you to reach beyond your comfort zone, challenging you to tap into your untapped potential. However, dreams alone are not enough. Dedication is the key that unlocks the doors to success. It is the unwavering commitment to your goals, the persistence to overcome obstacles, and the willingness to put in the necessary effort. Dedication connects your dreams to reality, transforming them from abstract aspirations into tangible achievements.

By surrounding yourself with sources of inspiration and positive influences, seeking out mentors, role models, and individuals who have achieved what you aspire to accomplish, you will develop the important characteristics it takes to win. Learn from their experiences, soak in their wisdom, and let their stories fuel your determination.

Never settle for complacency or mediocrity. Stay hungry for growth and continuously strive to become the best version of yourself. Embrace challenges as opportunities for personal development and view setbacks as lessons in resilience. Keep your eyes open to new possibilities and be receptive to the lessons that life presents.

Remember that the pursuit of your dreams is a lifelong journey. It requires patience, perseverance, and an unwavering belief in your abilities. Embrace the process, for it is through dedication and continuous effort that you will succeed.

Stay motivated and let your dreams and dedication be the driving force behind your every step. Embrace the person you aspire to become and work hard on your objectives. It will all pay off in the end.

Memo to Asha: May you stay motivated on your journey towards achieving your dreams. Remember, dreams and dedication are a powerful combination that can propel you forward, transforming your aspirations into reality. Stay driven, always seeking to grow into the person you have yet to become.

Lesson #59.

SUCCESS REQUIRES CONSTANT ADJUSTMENTS. BE OPEN TO CHANGE. BE OPEN TO STARTING OVER.

Life is filled with unexpected twists and turns, and the path to success is no exception. What worked yesterday may not work today, and what worked for someone else may not necessarily work for you. It is essential to remain adaptable and open-minded, ready to embrace new possibilities and explore different approaches.

Be willing to let go of outdated beliefs, habits, and strategies that no longer serve your growth and progress. Embrace change as a catalyst for transformation, understanding that it is through change that new opportunities arise. Stay curious, continuously seeking knowledge and learning from your experiences. Be open to new ideas and perspectives, as in doing so you will unlock your true potential.

Starting over is not a sign of failure but a testament to your courage and perseverance. It takes strength to acknowledge when something is not working and the willingness to take a step back, reassess, and make necessary adjustments. Starting over allows you to realign your goals, refine your strategies, and embark on a fresh journey towards success.

Throughout your journey, surround yourself with a supportive network of individuals who encourage and uplift you. Seek guidance from mentors who have navigated similar paths and have experienced the challenges of starting over. Their wisdom and support can provide valuable insights and help you navigate through the uncertainties.

Remember, that success is not a destination but a lifelong pursuit. It requires continuous growth, adaptation, and the ability to embrace change. Be flexible and agile in your approach, ready to pivot when needed. View setbacks as opportunities for a fresh start, and as potential steppingstones to a higher level of achievement.

Success requires the courage to embrace change and the willingness to start over when necessary. Embrace this mindset, my dear daughter, and let it propel you forward on your journey towards your dreams. May your openness to change and resilience in starting over guide you towards the success and fulfilment you deserve.

Embrace the process of constant adjustments with optimism and a growth mindset. Embrace change as a catalyst for personal and professional growth. Believe in your ability to adapt, to learn, and to thrive in the face of challenges. With each new beginning, you have the opportunity to create a brighter, more fulfilling future.

Memo to Asha: My dear, be always open to change and if you must, at one or multi points in your life, start over, may you do it with optimism and resolve. Success is not a linear journey, but a dynamic process that requires constant adjustments along the way. Embrace change as an opportunity for growth and be willing to start over whenever necessary.

Lesson #60.

OPPORTUNITY DOESN'T ALWAYS KNOCK.
Sometimes it whispers.

Opportunities often present themselves in the form of small moments, quiet whispers, or subtle nudges. They may come disguised as challenges, setbacks, or unexpected encounters. They require us to be present, to listen closely, and to trust our intuition.

In a world that values loud declarations and grand gestures, it is easy to overlook the gentle whispers of opportunity. We may become preoccupied with chasing after the big breakthroughs and dramatic moments, neglecting the small yet significant chances that lie right in front of us.

To seize these whispered opportunities, cultivate a sense of mindfulness and presence. Be attuned to the intricacies of the present moment and listen to the subtle cues that life provides. Trust your instincts and intuition, for they will guide you towards paths that hold hidden treasures. Maintain a curious and open mind, it is through these lenses that you will uncover the subtle nuances of opportunity. Be receptive to new ideas, different perspectives, and unexpected possibilities. Sometimes, the most transformative opportunities emerge from the unexpected and the unexplored. Remember that every experience, every encounter, and every challenge carry the potential for growth and opportunity. Approach each day with a sense of curiosity and a willingness to explore. Embrace the whispers of opportunity that come your way and be willing to take the necessary steps to pursue them.

Opportunities may require courage, resilience, and stepping outside of your comfort zone. They may demand you to overcome fear, doubt, and uncertainty. Embrace the challenges that accompany these whispered opportunities, for they are often the catalysts for personal growth and transformation. As you navigate through life, keep your senses attuned to the whispers of opportunity. Embrace the quiet moments, the subtle hints, and the unexpected turns.

Memo to Asha: My child, may you develop the awareness and discernment to recognize the whispers of every opportunity. Embrace the small moments, the subtle cues, and the unexpected encounters. Seize the opportunities that arise and follow through for a life filled with fulfillment, and endless possibilities.

Lesson #61.

FACING TODAY'S FEARS, REDUCES TOMORROW'S REGRETS.
Dare to Live out your dreams each and every day.

Fear has a way of holding us back, trapping us within the confines of our comfort zones. But when we allow fear to dictate our actions, we risk living a life defined by regret and missed opportunities. It is only by facing our fears that we can break free from their grip and unlock our true potential.

Each day presents a new canvas upon which you can paint the colors of your dreams. Embrace the courage within you to take bold steps towards what sets your soul on fire. Do not let fear immobilize you or hinder your progress. Instead, let it serve as a catalyst for growth and a reminder of the greatness that awaits on the other side. The road to success and fulfillment is paved with risks and challenges. But it is through these trials that we grow, learn, and discover our true capabilities.

Daring to live out your dreams requires a mindset of resilience, determination, and unwavering faith in yourself. It means accepting the uncertainty that accompanies the pursuit of your deepest desires. Embrace each day as an opportunity to push beyond your comfort zone, to pursue your passions with unwavering determination. Trust in your abilities, your strengths, and your capacity to overcome any obstacles that may arise along the way.

Do not wait for the perfect moment or the ideal circumstances. Seize each day as a gift, and let your actions align with your aspirations. Be ever open to the beauty of the present moment, for it is within this moment that your dreams can come to life. Do not let fear hold you back from living a life that is true to your authentic self. Face your fears with courage, knowing that on the other side lies growth, fulfillment, and a sense of purpose that transcends any regret.

Live each day as a testament of your strength, resilience, and unwavering commitment to live out your dreams. Embrace the challenges, embrace the unknown, and let your actions speak louder than your fears.

> *Memo to Asha: My child, by confronting the challenges that lie before you, you can minimize the regrets that may haunt you in the future. Dare to live out your dreams each and every day, embracing a life filled with purpose, passion, and fulfillment.*

Lesson #62.

COMFORT IS A FALSE FRIEND.
It will remind you of all your achievements
only to keep you right where you are. Keep elevating!

While achieving comfort is worthy of celebration, it can also be a seductive force that tempts us to settle into the familiarity of our current circumstances. Comfort creates a cozy bubble that shields us from the challenges and uncertainties of pressing forward. While it may provide temporary relief and a sense of security, it can also imprison us within a stagnant existence, preventing us from unlocking our full potential.

While it is important to celebrate your achievements and acknowledge the progress you have made, it's important to recognize that comfort and growth cannot coexist harmoniously. True growth lies beyond the boundaries of what is comfortable and familiar. It requires venturing into the unknown, embracing new challenges, and continuously pushing the limits of what you believe is possible. Do not let comfort become a barrier to your future success. Remember that growth and personal development thrive in the realm of discomfort. It is when you challenge yourself, take risks, and step outside your comfort zone that you truly flourish.

To keep elevating yourself, embrace a mindset of continuous improvement and never settle for mediocrity. Seek out new opportunities for learning and growth, even if they seem daunting or unfamiliar. Be willing to take calculated risks and embrace the discomfort that comes with stretching your limits.

Challenge yourself to set ambitious goals and strive for excellence in every area of your life. Break free from the allure of comfort and embrace the exhilaration of constant progress. Surround yourself with individuals who inspire and motivate you to reach higher and learn from those who have achieved what you aspire to accomplish.

Remember that life is a journey of constant evolution. Each day offers a new chance to surpass your previous accomplishments and take on the unknown with courage and determination. Be open to the discomfort that comes with growth, for it is through these moments of challenge and expansion that you discover your true potential.

> *Memo to Asha: My child, by confronting the challenges that lie before you, you can minimize and eliminate the regrets you will have in life. May you find the courage and strength to resist the false allure of comfort and keep elevating yourself to new heights. Remember, your potential is boundless, and your journey towards self-improvement is a continuous adventure.*

Lesson #63.

MONEY ANSWERS TO MONEY

Money has a way of gravitating towards itself, attracting opportunities and connections that can enhance your financial well-being. The wealthy and the rich understand the significance of engaging in business and partnerships within their own circles. They recognize the value of collaborating with like-minded individuals who share their vision and respect for money. Through these connections, they gain access to valuable knowledge, resources, and opportunities that can further propel their financial success.

It is not merely a matter of exclusivity or keeping secrets from the masses, but rather a shared stake in preserving and growing their wealth. By aligning themselves with individuals who also appreciate and understand the intricacies of money, the wealthy leverage their collective expertise to make informed financial decisions. They know where to find favorable deals, how to invest wisely, and how to pass on the wealth secrets they have accumulated to future generations.

Discipline is a crucial element when it comes to managing your finances. It involves cultivating healthy spending habits, saving diligently, and making wise investment choices. By exercising discipline, you can ensure that your money works for you, rather than being squandered or mismanaged. Educate yourself on the principles of finance and wealth accumulation. Learn from trusted sources, seek guidance from financial experts, and stay informed about the ever-evolving landscape of investment opportunities. Apply this knowledge to make sound financial decisions that align with your long-term goals.

Develop an uncompromising mindset of saving and investing for the future. Create a budgeting system that allows you to live within your means while also setting aside funds for savings and investments. By prioritizing financial discipline, you lay the foundation for a secure and prosperous future. Embrace the secrets of wealth, not for the sake of exclusivity, but as a means to secure your financial future and make a positive impact in your life and the lives of those around you. See money as a means to create opportunities, to invest in your dreams, and to support causes that align with your values.

Remember that money is not inherently good or evil—it is simply a tool that can be used to create opportunities and improve your quality of life. When you approach money with respect, knowledge, and discipline, you open doors to financial abundance and stability.

Memo to Asha: My child, may you embrace financial discipline and wisdom, my dear daughter, and may you unlock the secrets of wealth to create a life of prosperity, security, and fulfillment. Cultivate a mindset of abundance, always seeking opportunities to grow and prosper.

Lesson #64.

BE THE 'BOSS' OF YOUR LIFE.

'Boss' is more than a prevailing attitude.
It's a certain way of being.
Of quietly making power moves and winning at life.

To be the "boss" of your life means embracing the responsibility of setting limits. Understand your values, priorities, and goals, and establish clear boundaries that honor your well-being and align with your aspirations. Learn to say no to situations or commitments that do not serve your growth or contribute to your overall success. By setting limits, you create space for personal development, maintain balance, and protect your energy. Recognize the environments and situations that align with your goals and values, and confidently step into those spaces. Surround yourself with individuals who uplift and support your aspirations and seek out opportunities that challenge and inspire you. However, also trust your intuition and know when it is time to exit a situation or relationship that no longer serves your growth or well-being. Have the courage to let go of what no longer aligns with your vision and make room for new possibilities.

In your journey as the "boss" of your life, you will encounter various individuals who play different roles. Embrace the power to hire and fire people in and out of your life. Surround yourself with individuals who uplift, support, and believe in you. Seek out mentors, friends, and collaborators who inspire and challenge you to become the best version of yourself. However, be discerning and willing to let go of relationships that hold you back or negatively impact your progress. Surround yourself with those who contribute to your growth, and release toxic or unproductive connections that hinder your success.

Being the "boss" also entails setting high standards for yourself, taking accountability for your actions, and decisions, making power moves, winning and helping others win at life. Embrace the confidence and determination to pursue your dreams and goals relentlessly. Strive for excellence in all that you do, and let your performance speak for itself. By taking ownership of your journey, you will earn the respect of others and inspire them through your achievements.

Being the "boss" of your life is a lifelong commitment. It requires vision, self-awareness, courage, and resilience. Embrace this role with integrity, authenticity, and compassion. Lead by example, uplift others, and continuously strive for personal and professional growth.

Memo to Asha: My child, may you embrace the power of being the "boss" in your life and all the rewards and challenges it entails. May it empower you to set limits, seize opportunities, and create the life you were meant to live.

Lesson #65.

SUCCESS IS A NOMAD, IT KEEPS NO PERMANENT ADDRESS.

Stay hungry and humble.

Success is not a fixed destination or a permanent state. It is a journey filled with twists and turns, victories and setbacks. It is crucial to embrace the ebb and flow of this journey and understand that both the highs and lows are temporary. Just as success can find its way to you, it can also elude you at times. Remain humble, recognizing that life is unpredictable and that circumstances can change in an instant.

Remember that your achievements are not solely attributed to your own abilities, but also to the support and opportunities that have come your way. Appreciate the people who have helped you along the journey, and always extend a helping hand to others who may be facing challenges. Success is not solely about personal gain but also about lifting others up and creating a positive impact.

When you encounter moments of adversity or when success seems elusive, stay the course and maintain your resilience. Understand that setbacks are part of the journey and can provide valuable lessons and opportunities for growth. Instead of allowing disappointment or self-doubt to consume you, use these experiences as fuel to keep moving forward. Maintain your focus, adapt to new circumstances, and persevere with unwavering determination.

True success is not measured solely by external achievements or material wealth. It lies in the integrity, character, and growth that you cultivate along the way. Stay committed to your values, always striving to be the best version of yourself. Embrace a mindset of continuous improvement, learning from both success and failure, and let your journey be guided by authenticity and purpose.

Success is a transient visitor, and its presence in your life is not guaranteed. Stay grounded, show gratitude, and never lose sight of the lessons you have learned on your journey. Through the highs and lows, remember that your worth is not defined by external accomplishments but by the person you are and the positive impact you make in the world.

Memo to Asha: My dear, may you navigate the nomadic nature of success with grace and resilience. Embrace the humbling moments and stay the course with unwavering determination. Let your journey be marked by humility, authenticity, and a commitment to personal growth.

Lesson #66.

GOOD THINGS COME TO THOSE WHO WAIT, ONLY AFTER THE BETTER THINGS ARE TAKEN BY THOSE WHO WENT FOR IT.

Create your own luck. Have the courage to go for what you want, even when it seems impossible.

In life there are those who wait for their dreams to come to fruition, hoping that the universe will bring them what they desire. However, the truth is that the better things often go to those who take the initiative, who have the audacity to step outside their comfort zones and pursue their aspirations relentlessly.

Create your own luck by cultivating a mindset of determination and resilience. Believe in your abilities and have faith in your dreams. Be willing to put in the hard work, take risks, and push past your perceived limitations. Success often requires boldness and a willingness to face challenges head-on.

Do not be deterred by the fear of failure or the seeming impossibility of your goals. Remember that what may appear impossible is often just a reflection of limited thinking and lack of action. Break free from self-imposed limitations and embrace a mindset of possibility. Set audacious goals and pursue them with unwavering determination.

While it is essential to be patient and understand that success may not happen overnight, it is equally important to take consistent action towards your goals. Do not wait for the perfect moment or for everything to fall into place. Develop a clear plan, break it down into actionable steps, and commit yourself to taking those steps each day. Start where you are with what you have and make progress one step at a time.

Remember that your dreams and aspirations are valid and worthy of pursuit. Have the courage to go after what you want, even in the face of obstacles and naysayers. Surround yourself with people who uplift and support your ambitions and seek guidance from mentors who have achieved what you aspire to accomplish.

By embracing the mindset of action and seizing opportunities, you create your own luck. You shape your future and pave the way for the realization of your dreams. Believe in yourself, trust in your abilities, and let your determination and resilience lead the way.

Memo to Asha: My child, while patience is a virtue, waiting alone will not guarantee the fulfilment of your dreams. May you have the courage to go for what you want even when it seems impossible. Truth is, the better things often come to those who are proactive and seize opportunities, even in the face of challenges.

Lesson #67.

REMAIN OPEN TO CRITICISM AND BE EVER WILLING TO MAKE MISTAKES.

Remaining open to criticism is a vital aspect of personal and professional growth. It takes courage to listen to feedback, whether positive or negative, and to objectively assess its validity. Constructive criticism offers valuable insights and perspectives that can help you identify areas for improvement and refine your skills. Embrace feedback as an opportunity to learn and grow, even if it may be challenging to hear at times. At the same time, be willing to make mistakes. Recognize that mistakes are not indicators of failure, but rather steppingstones towards success. It is through mistakes that we learn valuable lessons, develop resilience, and gain a deeper understanding of ourselves and the world around us. Remain curious and steadfast on your journey, knowing that every mistake brings an opportunity for growth and self-reflection.

Venturing into new worlds and embracing change can be daunting. Breaking through the glass ceiling often requires stepping out of your comfort zone and taking risks. It is in these moments of discomfort and uncertainty that true growth occurs. Do not fear the possibility of failure or the judgment of others. Instead, cultivate a mindset of resilience and curiosity, knowing that every experience, successful or not, contributes to your personal and professional development.

Remember that life is a tapestry woven with both triumphs and challenges. Embrace the highs and the lows, the praise and the criticism, as they all contribute to your growth and transformation. Do not allow the fear of judgment or the opinions of others to hold you back. Trust in your own abilities and inner wisdom and let the lessons you learn along the way shape you into the extraordinary person you are meant to be.

Memo to Asha: My child, may you remain open to criticism and embrace the willingness to make mistakes. Remain open to the journey of self-discovery and continuous growth, knowing that each experience, both positive and negative, has the potential to mold you into a stronger and more resilient individual.

Lesson #68.

BE GREAT AT WHAT YOU DO AND MAKE NO APOLOGIES FOR YOUR WINS.

When you experience success, whether big or small, do not apologize for it. Embrace your greatness and strive to be the best version of yourself in everything you do. Celebrate your wins wholeheartedly and share your accomplishments with pride. It is essential to acknowledge your achievements and the progress you have made. Cultivate your skills, invest time and effort in honing your craft, and pursue excellence with unwavering determination. Allow your passion and dedication to shine through in every endeavor, knowing that your achievements are a testament to your hard work and commitment.

It is also important to remember that embracing your greatness does not mean diminishing the accomplishments of others. Instead, it is about acknowledging and accepting your unique gifts and using them to positively impact the world. Lift others up as much and as often as you can. Share your knowledge and experiences, and support those around you in their own pursuit of greatness. Collaboration and encouragement can foster a community of growth and success.

Do not let the insecurities of others hinder your progress or make you question your worth. Stay focused on your path and continue to develop your skills and talents. Surround yourself with individuals who uplift and support your aspirations, and distance yourself from those who may try to undermine your success. Remember that your journey is unique and that comparison with others serves no purpose other than to limit your own potential.

Always believe in your abilities and trust in your own potential. Do not be afraid to dream big, set ambitious goals, and pursue your passions with unwavering determination. Your success is not a threat to others but an inspiration for them to strive for their own greatness.

Memo to Asha: My child, I pray you become great in all your endeavors and your every win be recognized and celebrated. May your unique talents shine brightly and continue to grow and excel in all areas of your life.

Lesson #69.

MOST PEOPLE DON'T REALLY HAVE A MONEY ISSUE, THEY HAVE A MINDSET ISSUE.

The power of the mind is profound and transformative. Your thoughts, beliefs, and attitudes shape your reality and have a significant impact on your financial well-being. When your mindset is clouded by negativity, scarcity, and a limited perception of possibilities, it becomes challenging to attract abundance and create opportunities for financial growth. However, by consciously choosing to shift your mindset towards positivity, gratitude, joy, and determination, you open yourself up to a world of potential and unlock doors to success beyond imagination.

When you cultivate a mindset that sees challenges as a means to growth and learning, instead of viewing difficulties as roadblocks; and perceiving them as opportunities to develop resilience and find innovative solutions.

Recognize that there is an abundance of wealth and opportunities available to those who seek them. Refrain from prejudging people and opportunities, and instead approach them with an open mind, curiosity, and a willingness to explore their potential. Practice gratitude, my dear daughter. Be appreciative of the blessings and resources you currently have, regardless of their size or magnitude.

Gratitude cultivates a positive perspective and opens the doors to more abundance in your life. By focusing on what you have and expressing gratitude for it, you shift your mindset from scarcity to abundance and create a positive flow of energy that attracts greater financial prosperity.

Nurture joy on your journey towards success and wealth. Embrace a positive outlook, finding joy in the process of growth and achievement. Celebrate your milestones, both big and small, and let the joy of progress fuel your determination to keep moving forward.

Above all, maintain an unshakeable determination and deliberate discipline to win. Believe in your abilities, set ambitious goals, and persevere in the face of challenges. Develop a discipline that ensures consistent action and progress towards your objectives. Let your drive lead you to take purposeful steps every day, even when faced with obstacles or setbacks. With discipline, you build habits that contribute to your success and keep you focused on your path.

Remember, success and wealth are not solely determined by external circumstances, but by the mindset and beliefs you cultivate. Shift your focus from limitations to possibilities, from complaining to taking action, and from scarcity to abundance. Align your thoughts, beliefs, and actions always with an empowering mindset, and success and wealth will naturally follow.

Memo to Asha: *My child, strive always to embrace and nurture a mindset that is positive and attracts joy, success and wealth. Empower your mind with hope and optimism and let it guide you towards a future brimming with abundance, joy, and fulfillment.*

Lesson #70.

MONEY IS A REWARD FOR SOLVING PROBLEMS AND SUCCESS IS ITS SIDE EFFECT.

There is a myriad of ways to make money. The key is to use your mind beyond the extent of what most could perceive or achieve.

The ability to create wealth stems from your capacity to identify and address the needs and challenges of others. Instead of solely focusing on personal gain, direct your attention towards solving problems that impact individuals, communities, or industries. This requires innovative thinking, outside-the-box approaches, and a deep understanding of the desires and pain points of those you seek to serve.

Use your creative intellect to explore uncharted territories and discover opportunities where others may see obstacles. Cultivate an entrepreneurial mindset that is fueled by curiosity, tenacity, and the willingness to take calculated risks. Adopt a mindset that embraces continuous learning and growth, constantly seeking new knowledge and skills to enhance your problem-solving abilities.

Remember that success and wealth are not arbitrary, but rather earned through the value you bring to the world. Focus on providing unique and valuable solutions that meet the needs and desires of others. By doing so, you create a distinct position in the market and establish yourself as a trusted authority in your field.

Be ever open to the concept of abundance and collaboration, rather than doubt and competition. Seek partnerships and collaborations that amplify your impact and allow you to reach greater heights together. Surround yourself with like-minded individuals who share your greater vision and values, and together, you can create a ripple effect of positive change and financial prosperity.

In your pursuit of success and wealth, remember that it is not solely about accumulating material possessions but about making a meaningful difference in the lives of others. Focus on providing genuine values, fostering relationships built on trust and integrity, and cultivating a reputation as someone who consistently delivers exceptional results.

Believe in your ability to create wealth and success through problem-solving. Let your mind expand beyond the limitations of conventional thinking and embrace the infinite possibilities that lie before you.

Memo to Asha: My dear, may your quest be to contribute to the betterment of others and create a space for success that is uniquely yours. Embrace, always, your God-given gifts and abilities and apply them on your journey.

Lesson #71.

SUCCESS IS FOR THE COURAGEOUS.

*It doesn't matter who stands with you in battle,
If you're going to win, you'll need to learn to throw your
own punches.*

Success requires courage—the willingness to step outside of your comfort zone, face challenges head-on, and persevere in the face of adversity. It is not enough to rely on the support of others or wait for someone else to fight your battles. You must develop the self-belief and determination to take decisive action and make things happen.

Like a skilled fighter in the ring, you must learn to throw your own punches. This means taking responsibility for your own achievements and seizing opportunities when they arise. It means being proactive, resilient, and resourceful in pursuing your goals. Recognize that you have the power within you to overcome obstacles, navigate setbacks, and create your own path to success.

Success is not a passive endeavor. It requires a willingness to take risks, make difficult decisions, and persevere through challenges. Do not be afraid to embrace the unknown or face the possibility of failure. It is through these experiences that you will discover your true strength and resilience. Seek guidance and mentorship from those who have walked a similar path and can offer valuable insights. But always remember that, ultimately, it is up to you to take action and forge your own path.

Believe in your own abilities and trust in your intuition. Listen to your inner voice and follow the path that aligns with your values and aspirations. Trust that you have the skills, knowledge, and determination to overcome any obstacle that comes your way.

Be willing to face challenges head-on and take ownership of your journey. Embrace the courage within you, stand tall, throw your own punches, and fight for what you believe in.

Memo to Asha: My child, may you always be courageous and resilient on your path to success. Embrace the challenges that come your way, trust in your own abilities, and never shy away from putting in your own work and effort.

Lesson #72.

WATCH WHAT YOU DO REPEATEDLY AND HOW YOU SPEND YOUR TIME.

It's the little habits combined that make or break you.

Every choice you make, every action you take repeatedly, contributes to the person you become and the life you lead. Therefore, it is essential to be mindful of your habits and ensure that they align with your aspirations and values.

Your habits, whether big or small, have a cumulative impact on your overall well-being and success. Take the time to reflect on your daily routines and behaviors. Are they helping you progress towards your goals, or are they holding you back? Identify the habits that are beneficial and reinforce them, while being aware of those that may be detrimental and take steps to break free from them. Remember that success is not an overnight achievement, but a result of consistent effort and positive habits. It is through the accumulation of small actions performed consistently that you will see significant progress in your life.

Focus on developing habits that support your growth, health, and overall well-being. Pay attention to how you spend your time, as it is one of your most valuable resources. Be intentional with your time and ensure that it is aligned with your priorities and goals. Eliminate distractions and time-wasting activities that do not contribute to your personal or professional development. Cultivate habits that allow you to make the most of each day and bring you closer to the life you envision.

Be mindful of the choices you make on a daily basis. Even seemingly insignificant decisions can have a profound impact on your journey. Whether it is the choice to engage in a productive activity or to indulge in procrastination, each decision has the potential to shape your future.

Success is not solely determined by grand gestures or occasional bursts of effort. It is the culmination of the little habits and choices you make consistently. Be mindful of the power of your actions and embrace the opportunity to cultivate positive habits that will lead you towards the life you desire. Your daily actions and routines shape the course of your life, therefore cultivate positive habits that will propel you towards your goals.

Memo to Asha: My child, may you always watch what you do repeatedly and how you spend your time. Let the accumulation of positive and productive habits guide you towards the success and fulfilment you seek.

Lesson #73.

SUCCESS IN LIFE REQUIRES A GOOD NAME.

And trust is the ultimate measure!

A good name is built on a foundation of integrity, honesty, and consistency. It is not merely about how others perceive you but how you consistently conduct yourself, even when no one is watching. It is about aligning your actions with your values and consistently demonstrating ethical behavior in all aspects of your life.

Trust is the ultimate measure of your character and the key to building strong relationships. When others trust you, they are more likely to support you, collaborate with you, and rely on your capabilities. Trust is earned through your words and actions, by consistently demonstrating reliability, accountability, and authenticity.

Nurture your good name by staying true to your values and principles. Be conscious of the impact your choices and actions have on your reputation and the trust others place in you. Be a person of integrity, consistently doing what you say you will do, and honoring your commitments. Cultivate open and honest communication with others, fostering an environment of transparency and trust. Be genuine in your interactions, actively listen to others, and demonstrate empathy and understanding. Show respect for differing perspectives and always strive to maintain the trust that others have placed in you.

Remember that a good name and the trust of others are not acquired overnight but built through a lifetime of consistent character and honorable behavior. Be mindful of the choices you make and the impact they have on your reputation and relationships.

Strive to be a person of integrity in all areas of your life, both personally and professionally. Let your actions align with your values, and let your words be a reflection of your genuine and good intentions. By nurturing your good name and earning the trust of others, you will create a solid foundation for success and forge lasting connections that can support you throughout your journey.

Memo to Asha: My child, may you always prioritize your good name and strive to earn and maintain the trust of those around you. Your reputation and the trust others place in you are invaluable assets that can open doors, foster meaningful relationships, and lead to long-lasting success. Let your integrity and reliability be a light that guides you towards the fulfilling life you desire.

Lesson #74.

USE YOUR HARDSHIPS AS MOTIVATION TO SUCCEED.

It's not about who didn't show up for you.
It's about whether you'll SHOW UP FOR YOURSELF.

It is natural to feel hurt and discouraged when others let you down or fail to support you during difficult times. However, the key to triumph lies not in seeking validation or relying on others, but in finding the inner strength to persevere and show up for yourself.

Rather than allowing setbacks and disappointments to hold you back, use them as fuel to ignite your determination and drive. Let your hardships become a source of motivation to push beyond your limits and prove to yourself that you are capable of overcoming any obstacle.

Success is not dependent on the actions or presence of others, but on your own willingness to rise above adversity and pursue your goals with unwavering dedication. It is about cultivating a mindset that is focused on personal growth, self-belief, and resilience.

Take on the mindset of self-reliance and personal responsibility. Recognize that you have the power within you to shape your own destiny, regardless of the challenges you may face. Take ownership of your journey and commit to showing up for yourself every step of the way.

When faced with hardships, let them serve as reminders of your strength and resilience. Use them as catalysts to push yourself further, to set higher goals, and to strive for excellence in all that you do. Embrace the belief that every setback is an opportunity for growth and that every challenge is a chance to prove your resilience.

Remember that success is not about who didn't show up for you, but about your unwavering commitment to showing up for yourself. It is about finding the inner strength to rise above adversity, to persevere in the face of obstacles, and to relentlessly pursue your dreams.

Memo to Asha: My child, life is filled with challenges and disappointments, but it is how you respond to them that truly defines your character and determines your path to success. May you always find the inner strength to press forward. Instead of dwelling on who didn't show up for you, focus on showing up for yourself and embracing the opportunities that lie ahead.

Lesson #75.

THERE IS NO SUCCESS WITHOUT SCARS AND BRUISES.

Success is not solely measured by the absence of difficulties, but by the determination and resilience demonstrated in the face of adversity. Life has a way of testing us, pushing us to our limits, and leaving us with scars. The scars and bruises we accumulate along the journey should not be viewed as marks of weakness or failure, but as a testament of our strength and endurance. They are symbols of the battles we have fought and the lessons we have learned. They testify to our courage, perseverance, and growth.

Remember that success is not reserved for those who have led a painless and unblemished existence. It is for those who have faced adversity head-on, confronted their fears, and continued to persevere despite the challenges they encountered.

In the pursuit of success do not fear the scars and bruises that may come your way. Embrace them as part of your journey and use them as a source of motivation and inspiration. Let them remind you of the obstacles you have overcome and the strength you possess within.

Do not be discouraged by setbacks or deterred by temporary defeats. Instead, use these experiences as steppingstones toward your goals.

Let them fuel your determination and propel you forward. Trust in your abilities and have faith in the journey, for it is through the scars and bruises that we truly appreciate the sweetness of success.

Remember that success is not reserved for those who have led a painless and unblemished existence. It is for those who have faced adversity head-on, confronted their fears, and continued to persevere despite the challenges they encountered.

Nothing threatens your goals more than a lack of enthusiasm for starting and finishing something. Don't give in to it. Do not be discouraged by setbacks or deterred by temporary defeats. Instead, use these experiences as steppingstones toward your goals. Let them fuel your determination and propel you forward. Trust in your abilities and have faith in the journey, for it is through the scars and bruises that we truly appreciate the sweetness of success.

Life has a way of testing us, pushing us to our limits, and leaving us with scars. The scars and bruises we accumulate along the journey serve as reminders of our strength and endurance. But these scars should not be viewed as marks of weakness or failure. Instead, chey are symbols of the battles we have fought and the lessons we have learned. They testify to our courage, perseverance, and growth.

Memo to Asha: My dear, may you always embrace the challenges that come your way, knowing they are essential for your growth and eventual triumph. Let the scars and bruises you acquire along your path serve as badges of honor, testifying to your resilience and unwavering spirit.

Lesson #76.

DON'T WAIT FOR THE NEW YEAR TO START A CHANGE.

Any day can be a "New You" Resolution Day.

Imagine you have a blank canvas every morning when you wake up. It's like a brand new page in a book waiting for your story to be written. Now imagine the waste of space you would end up with if you skipped page after page to start filling it up in the middle. You don't need to wait for a special occasion or a particular date to make a change in your life. If there's something you want to improve, a dream you want to chase, or a goal you'd like to achieve, don't put it off until the next year begins. Start right now!

Remember, it's the small, consistent steps that lead to big transformations. So, if you want to eat healthier, start with a nutritious breakfast tomorrow. If you wish to learn something new, pick up a book or find an online course. And if you want to be kinder or more patient, practice those virtues with every interaction, starting today.

It's quite common for people to set resolutions as the calendar turns to a new year. There's this sense of a fresh start, a clean slate, and the excitement of new beginnings. But sometimes, the pressure to achieve these grandiose resolutions for the entire year can be overwhelming. It's like trying to climb a mountain in a single giant leap. That's where the beauty of everyday resolutions comes in. When you don't limit yourself to a once-a-year commitment, you take away that pressure. You realize that every morning when you wake up, you have the chance to be a better version of yourself, to grow, and to make positive changes. It's like having 365 opportunities in a year instead of just one.

Making lasting changes often requires time and effort. When you start on any random day, you're less likely to be discouraged by the enormity of a year-long commitment. You can break down your goals into smaller, manageable steps. Each day, you take one small step forward, and over time, those little steps add up to significant progress.

Memo to Asha: My dear, remember, life is a beautiful journey and each day is a precious gift. Don't let the idea of New Year's resolutions make you wait for the perfect moment to begin. Embrace the power of now, and watch how each day becomes an opportunity for growth and positive change.

Lesson #77.

YOU'VE MASTERED THE 'SELFIE', NOW MASTER YOURSELF.

In the age of social media, the mastery of the selfie often reveals a curated fragment of one's temporary self, meticulously posed and filtered to project a carefully constructed image to the world. This digital trend often used as a means to seek validation and external approval, or to momentarily boost one's self-esteem, remains rooted in the surface. Mastering oneself through real self-improvement achieving depth and meaning though embracing who you truly are, acknowledging your flaws and strengths, and committing to genuine personal growth. It transcends the ephemeral pursuit of fleeting admiration, focusing instead on long-lasting, meaningful transformation from the inside out.

While it is important to enjoy social interactions and celebrations, consider the following to help you improve yourself in other areas:

1). Reading is a powerful tool that can expand your knowledge, broaden your perspective, and fuel your imagination. Make time to indulge in books that inspire, educate, and empower you. Explore different genres and ideas and allow their revelations to shape your thoughts and actions.

2). Nurture yourself through exercise, proper nutrition, and adequate rest. Remember, a healthy body supports a healthy mind and spirit, enabling you to navigate life's challenges with greater resilience and clarity.

3). Cultivate self-control as it is the key to harnessing your true potential. Practice discipline in managing your time, emotions, and impulses. Be mindful of the words you speak, for they have the power to shape your reality and influence others.

4). Use your energy wisely and limit your idle time online and on social media. Instead, allocate that time to activities that nurture your personal growth.

5). Engage in practices that quiet the noise of the external world and allow you to connect with your inner self. Meditation provides a sanctuary of peace and introspection, enabling you to find clarity, balance, and spiritual time for self-reflection.

The allure of the selfie may capture a momentary spotlight, but the path of mastering oneself through authentic self-improvement shines with a lasting inner radiance, capable of enriching not only you but also the world you belong to. Embracing who you are and striving to become the best version of yourself is a journey worth embarking upon. It is what holds the promise of genuine fulfillment and enduring growth, beyond the confines of fleeting digital likes and comments.

Memo to Asha: My child, may you always prioritize your own growth and well-being. Nourish your mind, body, and spirit. Practice self-control and cultivate habits that promote personal improvement and productivity. Let the pursuit of real self-mastery be your foundation for a fulfilling and purposeful life.

Lesson #78.

IF IT DOESN'T EVOLVE YOU, THEN IT NEEDN'T INVOLVE YOU.

Time is expensive.
And how and where you spend it cannot be refunded.

Life is a constant journey of growth and evolution. Each experience, interaction, and decision should contribute to your personal and spiritual development. If something or someone does not align with your values, aspirations, or bring you closer to your goals, it may be time to reconsider their involvement in your life.

Remember that your time is limited, and once it is spent, it cannot be refunded. Therefore, it is essential to use it wisely and purposefully. Be discerning in your choices, and surround yourself with experiences and individuals who inspire, challenge, and support your personal evolution.

Evaluate the activities you engage in, the relationships you cultivate, and the commitments you make. Ask yourself if they align with your values and if they contribute positively to your growth. If they don't, have the courage to let go and make room for opportunities that truly nurture and elevate you.

Do not be afraid to prioritize your own growth and well-being. Set boundaries and allocate your time and energy to pursuits that align with your purpose and bring you joy, fulfillment, and personal evolution. By doing so, you create space for the people, experiences, and opportunities that will truly enrich your life.

It isn't selfish to prioritize your own growth and evolution. In fact, by investing in yourself, you become better equipped to serve and inspire others. So, be mindful of how and where you spend your time and ensure that it aligns with your personal values and aspirations.

Memo to Asha: My child, may you always be intentional in how you invest your time. Let the pursuit of personal growth and evolution guide your choices and let go of anything that no longer serves your higher purpose.

Lesson #79.

HAPPINESS IS THE GOAL. GROWTH IS THE JOURNEY.

*Live. Learn. Laugh. Love.
Leave a legacy.*

Live with a zest for life. Learn. Never stop growing. Embrace each day as an opportunity to explore, experience, and create memories. Seek out new adventures, take on challenges, and savor the simple pleasures that life offers. Live in the present moment, for it is in the present that you can truly experience the beauty and richness of life.

Throughout your life, aim to expand your knowledge and hone your skills. Be curious and open-minded, always seeking new perspectives and insights. Remember that wisdom comes not only from formal education but also from life experiences and the lessons they teach.

Laugh, for laughter is medicine for the soul. Find joy in the simple moments, share laughter with loved ones, and cultivate a sense of humor that can lighten even the darkest of times. Surround yourself with positive and uplifting people who bring deep contentment and joy to your life. Let laughter be your constant companion on this beautiful journey.

Love with all your heart. Nurture meaningful connections and relationships. Cherish the love you receive and give. Show compassion, kindness, and empathy to others. Love is a powerful force that can heal, inspire, and connect us all. Love yourself unconditionally, embracing both your strengths and imperfections.

Leave a legacy that extends beyond your own existence. Make a positive impact on the lives of others and contribute to the betterment of society. Use your unique gifts, talents, and passions to make a difference in the world. Whether it is through your work, relationships, or acts of kindness, leave an impact that inspires and uplifts future generations.

Memo to Asha: My dear, remember happiness is not a destination but a way of life. May you embrace this journey of growth, seeking out opportunities to live fully, learn continuously, laugh wholeheartedly, and love unconditionally throughout. May your life be filled with positive experiences and may you aspire always to leave a fulfilling legacy.

Lesson #80.

BE A STRONG WOMAN.

SAY NO. REJECT CALLS.
GET UP AND GO. CLOSE DOORS.
Deny second chances.

MAKE YOURSELF HAPPY.

Let your outer shell be made hard.
Not out of hurt, nor out of anger.
But out of your own FREE WILL.
To exercise your right to choose.
To change your mind 100 times.
To thrive, to live, to be happy.

To decide who you let in
And out of your world,
To simply BE.

By that very act you will uplift
The countless generations of women
Who couldn't fight, couldn't speak up,
Couldn't ASK QUESTIONS,
Who couldn't get an education,

Nor choose their own paths.
Who settled for second best.
Who were put down, quieted
Shamed, outcast,
Forced against their will.

FOR WANTING TO FREE
themselves and others.
And, even when while cooperative, to survive-
Received vile labels
And faced harsh consequences, still.

BE A STRONG WOMAN
For those who paid the high tolls
Set in place by an often feminine condemning,
oppressive society.

Who use sex as a tool,
View our STRENGTH as a threat
And deemed our voice unnecessary.

Throughout the world, and in our nation
Women stand with one conviction:
"You don't need a rhyme or reason,
GRANT YOURSELF YOUR OWN PERMISSIONS."

Be a strong woman for them,
Be a strong woman for yourself,
Be a strong woman for all future generations.

Lesson #81.

IT'S ALREADY IN YOU!

Everything you need to thrive, to heal to succeed, to change the world.

Everything you need to thrive, heal, succeed, and make a positive impact on the world is already within you. Believe in yourself, my dear daughter, for you are capable of achieving great things. You possess unique gifts, talents, and strengths that are waiting to be unlocked and unleashed. Embrace your power to shape your own destiny and create the life you desire. Trust in your abilities and have confidence in your innate wisdom. Recognize that you are limitless in spirit and capable of overcoming any obstacle that comes your way.

Healing, my dear daughter, starts from within. You have the power to heal yourself, both physically and emotionally. You have the power to thrive. Embrace the challenges that life presents and use them as opportunities for growth and transformation. Tap into your resilience, determination, and inner strength to navigate through difficult times. Trust in your ability to adapt, learn, and overcome.

Cultivate self-care practices that nourish your body, mind, and spirit. Listen to your intuition and honor your needs. Forgive yourself and others and let go of any burdens that weigh you down. Remember that healing is a journey, and you have the strength within you to embark on the most trying journey and emerge stronger and wiser.

Success is not an external measure but a deeply personal journey. Define your own version of success based on your values, passions, and aspirations. Set meaningful goals and work towards them with dedication, perseverance, and a growth mindset. Trust in your abilities and celebrate every milestone along the way.

Memo to Asha: My dear, remember that the power to thrive, heal, succeed, and change the world resides within you. Embrace it, nurture it, and let it shine brightly. Trust in yourself, believe in God and in your gifts, and never underestimate the impact you can make.

CHAPTER 5:

Lessons on People & Society

Lesson #82.

NOT EVERYONE IS GOING TO LOVE YOU. MOST PEOPLE DON'T EVEN LOVE THEMSELVES.

Not everyone is going to give you their trust, too many before you have broken it.

Many people in this world struggle to even love themselves. They carry their own insecurities, fears, and doubts, which can prevent them from truly accepting and loving others. Their inability to love you stems from their own internal battles, not from any deficiency on your part.

Trust doesn't come easy for many people. It is something that is earned over time. Don't expect it to be extended to you, especially by those who have experienced their trust being broken in the past. Understand that the actions of others who came before you may have created barriers and skepticism in the hearts of those you encounter. Do not take it personally, but instead, focus on consistently showing up with integrity and authenticity.

Likability is subjective and often rooted in people's own biases, preferences, and fears of the unfamiliar. Embrace your uniqueness and celebrate your differences, knowing that it is these qualities that make you who you are. Do not strive to fit into molds or conform to societal expectations, for true fulfilment comes from staying true to yourself.

Remain true to who you are. Embrace your individuality, trust in your own abilities, and love yourself unconditionally. Pursue your dreams and aspirations with unwavering determination and passion, not for the validation or acceptance of others, but for your own personal fulfilment and growth. Remember that your worth is not defined by the opinions or love of others. It is found within yourself, in the strength and beauty that resides within you. Embrace self-love, self-acceptance, and self-belief as your guiding principles. Let the love you have for yourself propel you towards your dreams and empower you to succeed on your own terms.

Memo to Asha: My child, may you always trust, love, and appreciate yourself enough to pursue your dreams. Always be ever willing to embrace your uniqueness, honor your worth, regardless of who does or does not love you.

Lesson #83.

YOU MIGHT MEAN WELL AND STILL HURT PEOPLE.

In our interactions with others, it is essential to approach every situation with empathy, kindness, and respect. However, despite our best efforts, misunderstandings, conflicts, or unintended consequences may occur. It is crucial to understand that impact holds greater significance than the best intent. Even if you did not mean to hurt someone, their pain is real, and it is important to validate their feelings and experiences.

When you become aware of the hurt you have caused, it's essential to take accountability and strive to make it right. Show empathy and actively listen to the person affected, seeking to understand their perspective and feelings. Offer a sincere apology, taking responsibility for your actions and acknowledging the impact they had.

Demonstrate genuine remorse and a willingness to learn and grow from the experience. Take proactive steps to rectify the situation and prevent similar harm from occurring in the future. This may involve making changes to your behavior, seeking education or guidance, and actively working towards personal growth and self-improvement. It is through consistent effort and reflection that we can learn from our mistakes and become more considerate and compassionate individuals.

Remember that our journey through life is a continuous learning process. None of us are perfect, and we will inevitably make mistakes along the way. However, it is our willingness to acknowledge our mistakes, take responsibility, and actively work towards making amends that truly defines our character.

Memo to Asha: My child, may you approach your every interaction with empathy; being mindful of the impact your words and actions can have on others. And when necessary, have the humility and courage to admit your faults and make things right. By doing so, you contribute to a world filled with understanding, healing, and growth.

Lesson #84.

PROTECT YOUR ENERGY SPACE LIKE IT WAS YOUR PRIVATE BEDROOM.

You have the power and the right to choose who occupies space in your life. You are under no obligation to give anyone a permanent place if they do not align with your values, aspirations, and overall well-being. Just as you would carefully select who enters your personal bedroom, it is crucial to verify and qualify those you allow access to your energy and inner world.

Surround yourself with individuals who uplift, support, and inspire you, and do not hesitate to release those who bring negativity and spiritual baggage. Your energy space is a sacred and precious resource. It is where your peace, joy, and growth flourish. Protect it fiercely. Be mindful of the company you keep and the relationships you invest in. Surround yourself with those who radiate positivity, authenticity, and love.

Be discerning when it comes to forming friendships and romantic relationships. Pay attention to the energy exchanges that occur. If you find that someone consistently brings negativity, drama, or drains your energy, it may be necessary to distance yourself from them. Remember that you deserve to be surrounded by people who add value to your life and elevate your spirit.

Strive, always. to nurture your inner peace and protect it from those who seek to disrupt it. Negative influences can derail your blessings and hinder your spiritual growth. Filter out those in your circle who do not uplift, inspire or contribute positively to your life. Choose relationships that support your personal and spiritual development and let go of those that no longer serve your highest good.

Remember that you are the gatekeeper of your energy space. It is your responsibility to create an environment that nurtures your well-being and aligns with your aspirations. Protect your energy space as you would your most cherished sanctuary and be mindful of who you allow access to it.

Memo to Asha: My child, may your world be filled with positivity, love, and alignment; and may you surround yourself, always, with individuals who lift you higher, support your growth, and contribute to your overall well-being.

Lesson #85.

PEOPLE FAIL THEMSELVES.
THEY CAN MOST CERTAINLY FAIL YOU.

Don't expect others to always keep their promises.
Put your highest trust in God and yourself alone.

While it is natural to desire trust and dependability in others, it is essential to remember that people are fallible beings. They may face their own challenges, make mistakes, or prioritize their own needs above their commitments to you. While disappointing, it is important to recognize that this does not diminish your worth or invalidate others' trust in you.

Instead of relying solely on others, strive to cultivate a deep and unwavering trust in God, first, and then yourself. Trust that God's plan is greater than any human's actions or promises. Seek guidance, solace, and strength through your spiritual connection, knowing that He will never fail you. Trust in your own capabilities, intuition, and inner wisdom to navigate through life's challenges and make decisions that align with your values and aspirations.

While it is important to build meaningful relationships and maintain trust with others, it is equally vital to have a strong foundation of self-reliance. Cultivate self-trust by honoring your own boundaries, values, and intuition. Take responsibility for your own happiness, success, and well-being, understanding that you have the power to shape your destiny.

By placing your highest trust in God, you free yourself from the disappointment and potential hurt that may arise from relying too heavily on others. You empower yourself to take charge of your own life, make decisions with confidence, and navigate challenges with resilience and grace. Remember that while people may fail themselves and fail you at times, it is not a reflection of your worth. Place your highest trust in the divine guidance of God and the strength of your own capabilities. With this foundation, you can overcome any obstacle and fulfil your purpose.

Memo to Asha: May your trust in God and in yourself be unwavering. Let it guide you through the ups and downs of life and empower you to embrace your calling in life at your highest and fullest potential.

Lesson #86.

ALWAYS BE A GOOD FRIEND.
RESPECT AND DO RIGHT BY ALL.

Friendship is a precious gift that enriches our lives and brings joy and support in both good times and bad. Cultivating and nurturing meaningful friendships are essential parts of leading a fulfilling and meaningful life. To be a good friend, it is crucial to approach relationships with respect and empathy. Treat others the way you would want to be treated, and always strive to do right by them. Show genuine interest in their lives, listen attentively to their thoughts and feelings, and be there to support them in times of need.

Respect is the foundation of any healthy friendship. Respect each person's boundaries, opinions, and individuality. Value their perspectives and differences, even when they may not align with your own. Embrace diversity and learn from others, as each person brings a unique set of experiences and wisdom to the table.

Communication is key in building and maintaining strong friendships. Be open, honest, and authentic in your interactions. Express your thoughts and feelings sincerely, while also being mindful of how your words may impact others. Effective communication helps to foster understanding, resolve conflicts, and deepen the bonds of friendship.

Part of being a good friend is being reliable and dependable. Show up when you say you will and follow through on your commitments. Your friends should be able to trust and count on you, knowing that you will be there for them when they need you most. Be supportive of their goals and dreams and celebrate their achievements as if they were your own.

Friendship is a two-way street, and it requires effort and investment from both sides. Take the initiative to reach out and spend quality time with your friends. Create opportunities for shared experiences, whether it's through outings, shared hobbies, or simply engaging in meaningful conversations. Cherish the moments you spend together and make lasting memories.

Like all relationships, the friendships we foster will at times encounter challenges and disagreements. It's important to approach these situations with understanding, patience, and a willingness to work through conflicts. Practice forgiveness and be open to growing together, as true friendships can withstand the tests of time and adversity.

Memo to Asha: My dear, being a good friend not only enriches the lives of those around you but also brings immense joy and gratification to your own life. Treat others with respect, be a reliable and supportive presence, and cherish the bonds of friendship that you cultivate. In doing so, you will create a network of love, trust, and companionship that will uplift and sustain you throughout your journey.

Lesson #87.

WHEN YOU'RE ON A WINNING MISSION, BE EVER READY FOR OTHERS' OPPOSITION.

As you strive for success and navigate the path to fulfill your mission, it is inevitable that you will encounter opposition along the way. Some individuals may feel threatened by your determination, achievements, and growth. They may harbor envy or resentment, leading them to act in ways that seek to undermine your progress.

Enemies may emerge seeking to hinder your journey or cast doubt upon your abilities. They may attempt to dim your light, sow seeds of discord, or challenge your accomplishments. It is essential to recognize that their actions stem from their own insecurities and fears. Their negativity is not a reflection of your worth or the validity of your mission.

Gossipers, too, may arise, spreading falsehoods and lies in an attempt to tarnish your reputation or diminish your achievements. Their words may carry the weight of malice and seek to undermine the trust and respect others have for you. It is crucial to remain steadfast in your truth, knowing that your actions and character speak louder than any rumors or falsehoods.

In the face of opposition, always strive to rise above. Stay focused on your mission, guided by your passion and purpose. Surround yourself with a supportive network of individuals who believe in you and your vision. Seek wisdom from those who have faced similar challenges and triumphed, drawing strength from their experiences.

Remember, the opinions and actions of others do not define your worth or the trajectory of your mission. It is up to you to stay true to yourself, your values, and your purpose. Embrace resilience, fortitude, and an unwavering belief in your abilities. Let their opposition serve as inspiration to excel, igniting an even greater determination to succeed.

Your focus should remain on the positive impact you are striving to make, rather than being consumed by the negativity of others. Surround yourself with positivity and let your actions and achievements speak for themselves. The energy you invest in your mission will ultimately drown out the noise of opposition.

Memo to Asha: My child, may you rise above any opposition and continue on your winning mission with unwavering determination, grace, and resilience. Trust in your abilities, believe in your purpose, and let the negativity of others serve as a reminder of your strength and resolve.

Lesson #88.

FAMILY IS OUR FIRST TASTE OF SOCIETY.

Some will support you, some won't.
Some care about you, some don't.
It doesn't matter what they think, do or say,
The toll is on you to make it anyway.

Our family units form the foundation of our lives. It is within these familial relationships that we first learn about love, support, and connection. However, it is also within the family unit that we encounter varying degrees of understanding and care. Some family members may wholeheartedly support your aspirations and dreams, while others may struggle to comprehend or validate your choices.

It is vital to recognize that the opinions and actions of others, even within your own family, do not define your worth or dictate the path you must take. While it can be disheartening to face indifference or lack of support from family members, it is essential to remain steadfast in your own beliefs and aspirations.

Your journey in life, dear daughter, is unique and deeply personal. It is not bound by the expectations or judgments of others, including those within your family. The toll of making your dreams a reality falls upon you alone. It is up to you to forge your own path, regardless of what others may think, do, or say.

Rather than seeking external validation or approval, turn inward and listen to the voice within you. Trust your instincts, embrace your passions, and pursue your dreams with unwavering determination. Surround yourself with a supportive network of individuals who genuinely care about your well-being and believe in your potential.

Remember, my dear daughter, that your worth is not contingent upon the approval or understanding of others, even within your family. Your journey is yours alone, and it is within your power to create the life you envision. Embrace your individuality, trust in your abilities, and rise above any negativity or lack of support that may come your way.

> *Memo to Asha: My child, you have the strength and resilience to make it. Trust in yourself, surround yourself with those who uplift and inspire you, and continue to pursue your dreams with unwavering determination. Your path may be met with various criticism from family, but ultimately, it is your journey to embark upon and your success to define.*

Lesson #89.

PROVE THEM WRONG. OR ACCEPT THEIR CRITICISM.

With society, all else is irrelevant.

Society can be a powerful force that influences our thoughts, actions, and perceptions. It often sets standards and expectations that may not align with our true selves or our unique aspirations. In the face of societal pressures, it is important to remember that your worth and fulfillment come from staying true to who you are and what you believe in. There may be times when you encounter doubt, skepticism, or criticism from society. People may question your choices, belittle your ambitions, or discourage you from following your dreams. It is in these moments that you have a choice—to either prove them wrong by achieving what they deemed impossible or accept their criticism while remaining steadfast in your path.

Proving others wrong requires resilience, perseverance, and unwavering determination. It means embracing the challenges, overcoming obstacles, and demonstrating through your actions that you are capable of achieving greatness. It means rising above societal expectations and refusing to be confined by the limitations others may impose upon you.

Alternatively, accepting their criticism can be an opportunity for self-reflection and growth. It means having the strength and wisdom to discern constructive feedback from baseless negativity. It means acknowledging the perspectives of others while staying true to your own values and aspirations. Accepting criticism does not mean conforming to societal norms or compromising your dreams—it means finding the balance between staying open to growth and remaining authentic to yourself.

Ultimately, the opinion of society is not what defines your worth or determines the course of your life. Your worth lies within you, and your journey is uniquely yours to navigate. Embrace your individuality, follow your passions, and let your actions speak louder than any criticism or doubt that may come your way. Trust in your abilities, stay focused on your goals, and surround yourself with those who support and uplift you. The validation and fulfillment you seek should come from within yourself, not from the opinions or judgments of society.

Memo to Asha: My child, may you embrace the strength within you, and let it propel you forward on your journey. Choose to prove others wrong, if it aligns with your aspirations and accept constructive criticism, if it contributes to your growth. But above all, remain authentic to yourself and follow the path that resonates with your heart and soul.

Lesson #90.

KEEP FLYING HIGH UNTIL OTHERS' NEGATIVITY CAN'T REACH YOU.

Negativity can come in various forms. It may manifest as criticism, doubt, or discouragement from those around you. It can be the result of jealousy, fear, or their own insecurities projected onto you. Whatever the source may be, it is essential to shield yourself from the toxic influence of negativity and continue to rise above.

Imagine that you are a majestic eagle soaring through the sky. Eagles fly high above the clouds, gliding effortlessly with grace and strength. They have a keen sense of vision and a powerful presence that commands respect. Like an eagle, you have the ability to soar above the noise and negativity, remaining untouchable by their harmful words or actions.

To keep flying high, it is important to cultivate a strong sense of self-worth and confidence in who you are and what you are capable of achieving. Surround yourself with positivity and supportive individuals who uplift and inspire you. Protecting your energy and mental well-being is crucial. Distance yourself from those who consistently bring negativity into your life. Surround yourself with individuals who celebrate your successes, offer constructive feedback, and genuinely care about your well-being. Set healthy boundaries to preserve your emotional and mental space and prioritize self-care to nurture your inner strength.

Remember that the negativity of others is a reflection of their own struggles and limitations, not a reflection of your worth or potential. Their words and actions do not define you. Keep your focus on your goals and aspirations, and let their negativity fall off as you soar higher.

Memo to Asha: *My dear, allow your resilience and strength be a shield against others' harmful words and actions. Embrace your inner power and continue to strive for greatness with unwavering determination and grace. May you fly high, until others' negativity can no longer reach you.*

Lesson #91.

RISE ABOVE THE MEDIOCRITY.

It's where the masses live and party.

Mediocrity represents the comfort zone where the masses reside. It is a place of complacency and conformity, where dreams are abandoned, and potential is left untapped. It is a space where individuals settle for less than what they are capable of achieving, simply because it requires less effort and commitment.

Know and believe that are meant for more. You possess a fire within you, a burning desire to make a difference and leave a lasting impact. It is through your relentless pursuit of excellence that you will elevate yourself above the mediocrity that surrounds you.

Rising above mediocrity requires courage and a willingness to challenge the status quo. It means setting higher standards for yourself and refusing to settle for less than what you deserve. It means embracing the discomfort of growth and pushing beyond your limits to achieve extraordinary results.

Embrace the mindset that while the masses may be content with mediocrity, you are called to something greater. Embrace your unique gifts, talents, and passions, and use them to propel yourself towards excellence. Surround yourself with like-minded individuals who share your drive for success and inspire you to push further. Remember, greatness is not achieved by following the crowd or seeking validation from others. It is forged through your own determination, perseverance, and unwavering belief in your abilities. Rise above the noise of mediocrity and chart your own path towards success and fulfillment.

As you strive for excellence, be prepared to make sacrifices and invest the necessary time and effort into honing your skills and mastering your craft. Always seek to improve and learn from every experience. Celebrate your successes, but never become complacent, as there is always room for growth and advancement.

Memo to Asha: *So, my dear daughter, let your light shine brightly and illuminate the path to excellence. Rise above the mediocrity that permeates society and inspire others to do the same. Embrace the challenges, embrace the discomfort, and embrace the journey towards greatness.*

Lesson #92.

NOT EVERYONE CLAPPING FOR YOU ARE YOUR FRIENDS. NOT EVERYONE CRITICIZING YOU ARE YOUR ADVERSARIES. TIME IS THE BEST REVEALER.

Be aware. Be open. Be wise.

In this journey called life, we encounter a multitude of individuals who play various roles in our experiences. Some are there to uplift and support us, while others may seek to take advantage of our kindness or diminish our achievements. It is essential to be aware and open, allowing time to reveal the true nature of those around us.

While it is natural to seek validation and praise from others, it is important to remember that not everyone who applauds your successes or offers kind words is genuinely invested in your well-being. Some may have ulterior motives or simply be drawn to your accomplishments without truly understanding or supporting you as an individual.

Similarly, not everyone who criticizes or challenges you should be seen as an adversary. Constructive criticism can be valuable and help you grow and improve. It is essential to differentiate between those who genuinely want to see you succeed and those who criticize out of jealousy, insecurity, or a desire to bring you down.

Time is a powerful ally when it comes to revealing the true intentions and character of those around you. It is through the passage of time that people's true colors become evident. Pay attention to how individuals consistently show up in your life, how they treat you in both good times and bad, and how their actions align with their words.

Be discerning, surround yourself with individuals who genuinely care for your well-being, support your growth, and uplift your spirit. Seek out those who celebrate your successes without envy, offer constructive feedback and stand by you through the ups and downs of life. As you navigate the complexities of relationships, remember to trust your instincts and intuition. They will guide you towards those who truly add value to your life and help you become the best version of yourself.

Be open to the lessons that different individuals bring, whether they are there to uplift, challenge, or criticize you. Each role is an opportunity for growth and learning. Above all, be wise in your interactions and relationships. Cultivate a deep sense of self-awareness and surround yourself with people who align with your values, inspire you, and genuinely care about your happiness and success.

Memo to Asha: *My dear, always be aware, open, and wise. Embrace the journey of discovering the true nature of the people around you. With time as your guide, you will build a circle of authentic and supportive relationships that enrich your life and contribute to your personal and emotional growth.*

Lesson #93.

WATCH WHAT THEY DO, NOT WHAT THEY SAY.

Even a broken clock tells the truth twice a day!

In a world where words can be easily manipulated and promises can be broken, it is essential to watch what people do rather than what they say. Actions, my dear daughter, speak louder than words and provide a more accurate reflection of a person's values, integrity, and reliability.

It is common for people to make grand promises or express intentions that may not align with their actual behavior. They may speak eloquently, make elaborate plans, and present themselves in a favorable light, but it is through consistent actions that the truth emerges. Pay attention to how individuals follow through on their commitments, how they treat others, and how they navigate challenges and adversity.

A person's actions reveal their true character and their level of authenticity. Do they practice what they preach? Do their actions align with their proclaimed values? Are they consistent in their behavior and choices? These are the questions to ponder as you evaluate the people in your life. While it is important to be discerning, it is also essential to recognize that actions can speak louder than words in both positive and negative ways. Sometimes, individuals may surprise us with their genuine care, compassion, and support, even if they may not express it in words. On the other hand, some may mask their true intentions with empty promises and persuasive language.

Remember that it is through consistent and observable actions that trust and credibility are built. Look for those who demonstrate integrity, empathy, and reliability through their actions. Surround yourself with individuals who not only speak words of kindness and support but also demonstrate these qualities in their everyday interactions.

As you navigate your relationships and encounters with others, be vigilant and attentive. Pay attention to the actions that speak volumes, as they reveal the true character of individuals. Allow time and consistent behavior to be the ultimate judge of someone's integrity and authenticity.

In a world where words can be deceiving, let the actions of others guide your judgments and decisions. Surround yourself with individuals whose actions align with their words, who consistently demonstrate kindness, compassion, and respect. Trust your instincts and intuition, as they will often lead you in the right direction.

Memo to Asha: My dear, remember actions speak louder than words. Always watch what others do, observe their consistency, and let their actions be the basis of your judgments and assessments. In doing so, you will be able to find and surround yourself with genuine, trustworthy, and reliable individuals who will enrich your life as you do theirs and contribute to your growth.

Lesson #94.

BE CONSISTENTLY YOU.

*Never let imitation make you question
the power of your own authenticity.*

You are a one-of-a-kind individual with a unique set of talents, perspectives, and experiences. Your authenticity is what sets you apart from the crowd and allows you to shine in your own remarkable way. Embrace it, celebrate it, and never let anyone or anything make you doubt its power.

Imitation may seem tempting at times, especially when we witness others gaining attention or praise for their actions or behaviors. It is natural to wonder if we should mimic their ways in order to achieve similar success. However, I want you to remember that true success and fulfillment come from embracing and expressing your own authentic self.

When you imitate others, you dilute the power of your unique voice and gifts. You rob the world of the beauty that only you can bring. Your authenticity is a gift, and it is through embracing and sharing it that you can make a lasting impact and create meaningful connections.

It is important to recognize that your authenticity is not dependent on external validation or comparison. You do not need to imitate others to prove your worth or gain acceptance. Your value lies in being unapologetically yourself, embracing your strengths, acknowledging your weaknesses, and growing into the best version of who you're meant to be.

When you stay true to yourself, you radiate a sense of confidence and authenticity that is magnetic. You attract people who appreciate and value you for who you are, not for who you try to imitate. Your unique perspective and experiences bring a fresh and valuable contribution to the world, and it is in honoring your authenticity that you can truly make a difference. Remember that authenticity is a journey, not a destination. It requires self-reflection, self-acceptance, and the courage to express your true self in every aspect of your life.

Surround yourself with people who celebrate your authenticity and inspire you to be even more true to yourself. Embrace your quirks, celebrate your passions, and honor your own voice. Your authenticity is a source of strength and power that will guide you towards a life filled with fulfillment, joy, and meaningful connections. Never let the imitation of others make you question the incredible value and impact of your own authentic self.

Memo to Asha: Be consistently you, and never underestimate the power of your authenticity. Embrace it, nurture it, and let it be the guiding force in everything you do. The world needs your unique perspective and contribution, and it is through embracing your authenticity that you will leave an indelible mark on the lives of others.

Lesson #95.

BE CAREFUL WHO YOU SHARE YOUR PLANS WITH AND TAKE ADVICE FROM.

While it is natural to seek guidance and support from others, it is essential to exercise caution and discernment. Not everyone who offers advice has your best interests at heart. Some may be driven by their own motives or self-interest, leading them to offer guidance that may not align with your goals or values.

Be mindful of those who are quick to offer advice without understanding the full context of your situation or the depth of your aspirations. They may lack the necessary knowledge or experience to provide meaningful guidance. It is important to remember that the path to success is unique for each individual, and not everyone is qualified to give you directions.

Additionally, be aware of envious friends who may take advantage of your trust and use it as an opportunity to sow doubt and negativity. These individuals may project their own fears and limitations onto you, discouraging you from pursuing your dreams and ambitions. It is important to recognize their intentions and shield yourself from their negative influence.

Question every word and filter every counsel. Evaluate the source of advice and consider their track record, values, and achievements. Surround yourself with individuals who have demonstrated wisdom, integrity, and success in their own lives. Seek guidance from those who genuinely support and uplift you, and who have your best interests at heart. The decisions and actions you take are, ultimately, your own responsibility. Trust your instincts and intuition, and never let the doubts and negativity of others overshadow your dreams. Remember that you have the power to shape your own destiny and that your success is not determined by the opinions and advice of others.

Be selective about who you share your plans with, my dear daughter, and be cautious about whose advice you accept. Seek guidance from those who have a proven track record of success, who inspire and support your growth, and who genuinely want to see you thrive. Surround yourself with individuals who uplift and encourage you to reach your full potential. Always remember that you have the inner wisdom and strength to make the right decisions for yourself. Trust your own judgment and be confident in your ability to navigate your path to success.

Memo to Asha: My dear, learn to question every word, and filter every counsel. Protect your dreams, trust your instincts, and surround yourself with those who genuinely support and believe in your potential. With wisdom and discernment, you will navigate the journey of life with clarity and confidence.

Lesson #96.

DON'T WASTE YOUR LIFE ENVYING OTHERS' JOY OR ACCOMPLISHMENTS.

God is the giver of all gifts and talents. Look to uncover and activate your own. They may still be giftwrapped.

Envy is a thief that robs us of joy and contentment. When we focus too much on comparing ourselves to others and longing for what they have, we lose sight of our own journey and the blessings that await us. Instead of dwelling on what others have achieved or attained, shift your focus inward and explore the untapped potential within you.

Just as gifts are often wrapped in beautiful packaging, your own gifts and talents may still be hidden, waiting to be uncovered and developed. Embrace the process of self-discovery and embark on a journey of self-exploration to uncover the unique gifts that reside within you. Take the time to reflect on your passions, interests, and the activities that bring you joy and fulfillment.

It is through self-reflection and self-awareness that you can begin to activate and nurture your own gifts. Engage in activities that align with your interests, seek opportunities to learn and grow, and surround yourself with individuals who inspire and support your journey of self-discovery. Remember, my dear daughter, that your gifts are meant to be shared with the world, and by cultivating them, you can make a meaningful impact.

While it is natural to admire and appreciate the achievements and talents of others, do not let envy consume your thoughts and actions. Instead, use the success and accomplishments of others as inspiration and motivation to unlock your own potential. Celebrate the joys and accomplishments of others without comparing them to your own journey. Each person's path is unique, and your time will come to shine in your own special way.

Trust in God's timing and plan for your life. He has bestowed upon you specific gifts and talents that are waiting to be discovered and utilized for a purpose greater than you can imagine. Embrace the process of uncovering your gifts and remember that comparing yourself to others only hinders your own growth and progress.

Memo to Asha: My dear daughter, do not waste your precious life in envy. Instead, focus your energy on uncovering and developing your own gifts and talents. Trust in the divine plan for your life and have faith that God has equipped you with everything you need to fulfill your purpose.

Lesson #97.

YOUR ENEMY ISN'T THE PROBLEM.

It's the power you give them that is.

Often, we attribute great power to our enemies or those who may wish us harm. We allow their words, actions, and opinions to affect our emotions, self-esteem, and overall well-being. But I want you to remember that their power over you is only as strong as the power you grant them.

Instead of viewing your enemies as insurmountable obstacles, shift your perspective and see them as opportunities for growth, resilience, and self-reflection. It is through these challenging encounters that you can cultivate strength, wisdom, and emotional maturity.

When you give power to your enemies, you relinquish control over your own life and allow them to dictate your thoughts, emotions, and actions. It is important to recognize that their negativity and hostility stem from their own insecurities, fears, and shortcomings. By understanding this, you can detach yourself from their influence and maintain your own sense of peace and inner strength.

Focus on building your own character, nurturing positive relationships, and pursuing your goals and dreams. Surround yourself with individuals who uplift and support you, and channel your energy into personal growth and self-improvement. By doing so, you diminish the power that your enemies hold over you and empower yourself to rise above their influence. Remember that your worth and identity are not defined by the opinions or actions of others. Your true power lies in how you respond to adversity and how you choose to live your life.

Stay rooted in your values, maintain a strong sense of self-worth, and let go of the power you have given to your enemies. Do not allow negativity, hostility, or the presence of enemies to consume your thoughts and energy. Instead, focus on cultivating a positive mindset, nurturing your own personal growth, and surrounding yourself with love, support, and understanding. Redirect your focus towards your goals, aspirations, and the positive impact you want to make in the world.

Memo to Asha: *My dear, may you have the strength within you to rise above any challenge. Release the power you have given to your enemies and reclaim control over your own life. Remember, it is not your enemies that define you, but the strength and grace with which you navigate the path before you.*

Lesson #98.

3 THINGS TO ASK OF THOSE YOU CALL YOUR FRIENDS AND BUSINESS PARTNERS:

That you make each other better.
That you make each other happy.
That you make each other wealthy.

When it comes to the relationships you form, whether they be friendships or business partnerships, it is crucial to set certain expectations and standards. Here are three important things to ask of those you call your friends and business partners:

1. Make each other better: Surround yourself with individuals who inspire and challenge you to become the best version of yourself. Seek friends and partners who uplift and support your growth, while also pushing you to reach new heights. Together, you can motivate one another to continuously learn, improve, and evolve. Through constructive feedback, shared knowledge, and mutual support, you can create an environment that fosters personal and professional growth.

2. Make each other happy: Cultivate relationships that bring joy, positivity, and fulfillment into your life. Surround yourself with

people who genuinely care about your well-being and happiness. Choose friends and partners who celebrate your successes, share in your joys, and provide a sense of comfort and support during difficult times. Together, you can create a sense of happiness and fulfillment that enhances your overall well-being.

3. Make each other wealthy: In the realm of business partnerships, it is essential to collaborate with individuals who share your vision for success and are committed to achieving financial prosperity. Seek partners who bring complementary skills, expertise, and resources to the table. Together, you can leverage each other's strengths and work towards mutual financial success. By aligning your goals, strategies, and efforts, you can create opportunities for wealth creation and abundance.

While these three factors—making each other better, making each other happy, and making each other wealthy—may be important considerations in your relationships, it is also important to ensure that your connections are built on trust, integrity, and mutual respect. Communication, transparency, and a shared sense of purpose are key ingredients in fostering meaningful and successful relationships.

Remember, relationships are a two-way street. Just as you have expectations of others, be prepared to meet those expectations yourself. Strive to be a supportive, uplifting, and inspiring friend and partner. Nurture a mindset of collaboration, empathy, and generosity.

Surround yourself with individuals who align with your values, goals, and aspirations. Choose friends and partners who bring out the best in you, contribute to your happiness, and help you progress towards financial abundance. that can propel you towards personal and professional success.

> *Memo to Asha:* My dear, always trust your intuition and be discerning in selecting the people with whom you share your time, energy, and aspirations. Surround yourself with those who embody the qualities and values that you hold dear. Together, you can create meaningful and mutually beneficial relationships that elevate and empower each other.

Lesson #99.

PLAY NICE.

The world is a very small town. Eventually, you meet everyone you helped or hurt a second time around.

Imagine that the world we live in is like a tightly knit community, where each person you encounter has the potential to cross your path again. Actually, you do not have to imagine, it's simply true. Every interaction, whether positive or negative, leaves an imprint that resonates through time and though we may not be able see its eternal effects, it is there. When you extend kindness, compassion, and support to others, you sow seeds of goodness that will bloom in your future encounters. Conversely, when you cause harm or inflict pain, those echoes of your actions can reverberate back to you when you least expect it. Everything we do, every decision we make, has the potential to circle back to us, presenting us with opportunities for growth and redemption. But, just the same, the person you hurt today may become a formidable stumbling block or mirror reflecting the consequences of your actions.

Do not be fooled into thinking that you can escape the repercussions of your choices. What you get away with today may not stay away forever. Integrity, honesty, and compassion are virtues that transcend time and space. They create a foundation of trust, respect, and goodwill that can withstand the test of time.

Therefore, be mindful always, of the impact you have on the lives of those around you. Your words, your gestures, and your choices hold immense power. Treat others with respect and empathy, for the energy you put out into the world will find its way back to you.

In this intricate dance of life, we must embrace the power and responsibility that lies within each of us. Strive to make a positive impact, leaving behind a trail of kindness and love in your wake. Treat others with dignity, even in moments of disagreement or conflict. Seek forgiveness when you falter and extend it to those who seek it from you. Embrace the knowledge that your actions matter, and through conscious living, you can shape the world around you.

Memo to Asha: Remember, my dear, that the world may seem vast, but it is truly a small town. Your choices, your actions, and your intentions have the power to reverberate through time and touch the lives of those around you. Play nice, my love, for what you sow in the hearts of others will find its way back to you, creating a life of depth, connection, and fulfillment.

www.ingramcontent.com/pod-product-compliance
Lightning Source LLC
Chambersburg PA
CBHW060916120626
46553CB00001B/352